Getting Started
with
University-Level
Work Based Learning

Getting Started
with
University-Level
Work Based Learning

Edited by
Alan Durrant
Garth Rhodes
David Young

Middlesex
University
PRESS

First published in 2009 by Middlesex University Press

Copyright © Middlesex University Press

ISBN 978 1 904750 70 3

A CIP catalogue record for this book is available from The British Library

Cover design by Helen Taylor
Typesetting by Carnegie Publishing Ltd
Printed in the UK by Ashford Colour Press

Middlesex University Press
Fenella Building
The Burroughs
Hendon
London NW4 4BT
Tel: +44 (0)20 8411 4162: +44 (0)20 8411 4161
Fax: +44 (0)20 8411 4167
www.mupress.co.uk

Published with the support of the
Centre for Excellence in Work Based Learning

Middlesex
University

Foreword

This compact volume is designed for learners in the workplace who are studying at university level and designing some – or all – of their studies to reflect the practices, issues and concerns of their workplaces.

Organised in five sections, the book covers all aspects of university level work based learning (WBL). It begins by exploring the value of WBL and some of its characteristics to offer support in deciding if this is the approach for you in your studies. It then discusses initial steps in university-level work based study and moves on to offer some advice on planning, thinking, reflecting and undertaking assessment. It also considers the kinds of support you might need – and expect to have access to. Presented as a series of questions, the book is designed to be a reassuring quick reference for learners in the workplace.

Written by university tutors who are experienced in supporting work based learners undertaking such programmes of study, the book is designed to offer reassurance and initial guidance and signposting to those about to embark on this challenging, yet exhilarating learning journey.

Professor Freda Tallantyre
Higher Education Academy
February 2009

List of Contributors

Sue Bennett
Work-related Learning
Development Officer
Northumbria University

Alan Durrant
Head of Work Based Learning
School of Arts and Education
Middlesex University

Ann Minton
Workforce Development Fellow
and Principal Tutor in Work Based
Learning
University of Derby

Chris Newman
Learning Through Work
Development Co-ordinator
University of Derby

Steve Partridge
Senior Lecturer in Work Based
Learning
School of Health and Social
Sciences
Middlesex University

Alison Pringle
Work-related Learning
Development Officer
Northumbria University

Garth Rhodes
Head of Flexible Learning Centre
School of Health, Community &
Education Studies
Northumbria University

Tracey White
Senior Lecturer in Work Based
Learning
University of Derby

Professor David Young
Head of Flexible Learning
School of Flexible and Partnership
Learning
University of Derby

Contents

INTRODUCTION:

The Book at a Glance

Our working sub-title for this book as we put it together was:

'All the answers to all the questions you will ever ask about university-level work based learning to make it work for you.'

Not exactly a snappy title, is it? So you can see why we decided not to run with it! And 'all the answers to all the questions' is slightly tongue in cheek (it's not a very long book, after all). Nevertheless, it gives a clue to our reasons for writing it.

Those of us involved in work based learning (WBL) have, over the last few years, met each other on working groups and at conferences concerned with work based learning, as external examiners, as co-authors and so on. Over coffee and other refreshments, conversation often involved sharing stories and anecdotes about work based learners and the kinds of practical advice they and we had found useful.

So this book came about. Designed, not as an encyclopaedia – that would set up unrealistic expectations – but as an easily accessible compendium or learners' guide to university-level WBL programmes. It's not a study skills manual, although there is some advice about studying. It's not a critique of the theoretical basis of work based learning, although we do say something about the principles behind such learning. It's intended to support you if you're beginning or even just thinking about work based learning, and also to be a companion throughout your studies.

We did think about making an electronic resource, but we weren't sure exactly where it might sit online and, despite their constantly increasing portability you won't necessarily have your computer switched on when you have a question, so in the end we went for a book. It's small enough to carry in a pocket or bag, but not as thin and disposable as a leaflet. We hope you find it useful.

We've organised the book in five main sections. Each section asks a series of questions and offers some answers. There are two sorts of answers: short answers and more detailed responses which offer greater food for thought and more ideas for you to consider. We also offer case studies and the views of real work based learners, although we don't use their actual names and the companies they work for are anonymised too.

While we hope you're going to take time to absorb the detail, we know that you won't always do this. So here, at the beginning of the book, as promised, are all the short answers to all (or most of) the questions you'll ever need to ask about negotiated university-level WBL to make it work for you, together with page references for the detail.

Short answers to all (or most of) the questions

Why choose WBL?

Because it will help you to be more informed and more effective at work.

For a more detailed response see page 1.

What do we mean by WBL in higher education?

University-level learning, which takes as its starting point you and your activities at work in your company or organisation.

For a more detailed response see page 1.

Is it worth it?

A very definite 'yes'! Of course, we would say that. Don't just take our word for it, though. Read any of the case studies and comments from learners in the main sections of the book.

For a more detailed response see page 2.

What is the status of a WBL qualification?

Exactly the same as any other university-level qualification because, in achieving your qualification, you'll face the same level of intellectual challenge and rigour as learners on more traditional courses.

For a more detailed response see page 3.

Who else has done this kind of university qualification?

Lots of people – and their numbers are increasing. In 2009, more than 30 universities were working to make their qualifications more accessible to learners in the workplace.

For a more detailed response see page 3.

What experiences have the learners had?

You can't generalise, any more than you could with any other group of learners. But most work based learners will have thought critically about changes in their workplace and have been supported in undertaking and reporting on at least one work based project.

For a more detailed response see page 5.

What are the likely benefits and drawbacks for me?

There are more benefits than drawbacks. Lots of work based learners say that their studies have made them more confident at work. Drawbacks might be that you become questioning of everything and get very involved in the process. Of course, you might see these as benefits!

For a more detailed response see page 8.

What are the likely benefits and drawbacks for my employer?

Employers like WBL; it's a great way for them to improve their business, develop their employees and to make their organisations work more effectively.

For a more detailed response see page 10.

Is it easy or is it really difficult?

It's challenging. Sometimes things will just slot into place, at other times, none of it will make sense. But all worthwhile activities are like that.

For a more detailed response see page 13.

What will I get at the end of it?

Your personal achievement will be marked by a university qualification which has national recognition and which, because it's based on work, offers benefits for your employer too.

For a more detailed response see page 15.

What do we mean by employer, employment and learner?

We have a very wide definition of what counts as 'work'. It's not just salaried employment, but any kind of purposeful activity. An employer could be the business or person for whom you work, or your line manager – or even yourself if you're self-employed. Throughout the book, we've used the term 'learner', rather than 'student' or 'participant' to refer to the person actually engaged in WBL.

For a more detailed response see page 18.

What are the principles of WBL in higher education?

We want to recognise higher learning wherever it has taken place and reward those who have achieved it with university qualifications.

For a more detailed response see page 21.

What does it mean to be a work based learner in higher education?

As a work based learner in higher education, you'll almost certainly have experience and expertise as a worker. You'll be taking your work activities and using them as the starting point for your studies.

For a more detailed response see page 23.

What are the differences and similarities between WBL and traditional higher education?

The similarities are that university level WBL is at the same standard as traditional higher education and you'll develop and use the same higher-level skills. The difference is that, in WBL, the focus is on the many different kinds of knowledge, which you use at work, and their application to your work practice, rather than on a single subject.

For a more detailed response see page 24.

Isn't WBL just the same as NVQ?

No. National Vocational Qualifications (NVQs) are work related and competence based. They reflect the skills and knowledge needed to do a job. University-level WBL on the other hand, looks to reflect the capability of skilled people in the workplace to handle the unfamiliar and unexpected.

For a more detailed response see page 25.

How will I start?

Usually by taking stock of your current situation as a worker and using this starting point to plan your way forward as a learner.

For a more detailed response see page 27.

Who will teach me?

Maybe a better question might be: 'How will I learn?' (See next question.)

How will I learn?

That's better! WBL is less about being instructed or passively receiving information and more about being an independent learner.

For a more detailed response see page 29.

What will I learn?

Essentially, you'll learn a new and higher level grasp of your practice and to manage and take responsibility for your own work and learning priorities.

For a more detailed response see page 30.

What are the ethical issues and principles in WBL?

Ethics is essentially about behaving in a 'right' or morally appropriate way. In WBL, working ethically means showing consideration for those in the workplace who are involved in your studies and being aware of how you deal with issues of confidentiality relating to the information you may collect and use in assignments and projects.

For a more detailed response see page 34.

What does it mean to be an independent learner?

It means assuming responsibility – in the case of university-level WBL usually with tutorial support – for planning, managing and reflecting on your learning.

For a more detailed response see page 39.

What does it mean to be a critical thinker?

Critical thinkers are self conscious about considering things for themselves, raising their own questions, finding supportive information for themselves and reaching and recording their own judgements.

For a more detailed response see page 40.

What does it mean to be a reflective learner?

For work based learners, reflective learning involves recalling the detail of work based activities after the event, evaluating their positive and negative aspects and showing how your new awareness will inform your future actions.

For a more detailed response see page 40.

How will I be assessed?

Various assessment methods are used including practical projects focused on your work, research investigations and their outcomes, management and technical reports, presentations and portfolios or collections of work completed through the course of the programme.

For a more detailed response see page 42.

Who is involved in my work based learning programme?

You! And then your tutor(s), people in your workplace, your family and friends and often other learners.

For a more detailed response see page 49.

What is expected of me?

Planning followed by sustained effort and commitment of time.

For a more detailed response see page 49.

Are there any particular skills I need to have?

You'll need to be organised and flexible in your thinking to work out what blend of work, study and personal life you feel comfortable with. But don't feel alone, and remember, you can always ask for help.

For a more detailed response see page 50.

How well motivated am I?

Only you know. But to succeed, you'll have to be motivated to work independently to manage and organise your own learning within a university programme.

For a more detailed response see page 52.

How will I fit this into my life?

There's no question that you will have to manage and juggle conflicting demands. Although WBL is based on your professional life, to succeed, you'll need to do more than sit at your desk. In addition to the hours you spend at work, you can maybe expect to spend the equivalent of a couple of evenings a week or a half-day at weekends.

For a more detailed response see page 52.

What is expected of my family and friends?

You'll need their understanding. It may be helpful to tell people around you – colleagues, family and friends – that you have made a commitment to study. This will not always remove or resolve conflicting demands on your time, but it can help.

For a more detailed response see page 55.

What can I expect of my employer?

Obviously it will vary widely, but speak nicely to them – and remind them that your university study is work based and so they will benefit from your studies as well as you.

For a more detailed response see page 57.

What if I am self-employed?

Speak nicely to yourself!

For a more detailed response see page 60.

What support can I expect from the university?

The university will be a starting point for your WBL studies – and a finishing point, as they will award you the qualification you seek. In between you can expect access to advice, expertise and resources to support your learning.

For a more detailed response see page 60.

Understanding universities

If you want to know more of the ins and outs of universities and their systems, then the short answers provided up to this point are unlikely to satisfy you. Chapter 5 deals with these issues in some detail. Go to pages 61–3 to find answers to the following questions:

- What does all the jargon mean?

- How do I choose the right university and programme for me?

- What's in it for my employer?

- Can I learn at a distance?
- Can I mix distance learning with study on the university campus?
- Will my previous study be recognised?
- Does the university have a lot of experience with work based learning?
- What are the different sorts of routes I could follow?
- Can I get a professional qualification through work based learning?
- Will I have to buy lots of books and other materials?
- What do I do if things go wrong?
- What are the consequences if I have problems coping with the course?

Other questions

- What does it cost?
- Who pays?
- Does the government contribute money towards my work based programme?
- Working for a large employer?
- Working for a small company or organisation?
- Self-employed?
- How do I get the correct fees information?
- How are fees calculated?
- Where do I go for information on financial support?
- Am I eligible for a grant?
- Am I eligible for a loan?
- Am I eligible for a bursary or scholarship?
- What additional guidance is available to me about financial support?
- So how do I handle getting the right information?

So, now you know all you need to know about work based learning...

Still have some questions? Well, that's good, because the whole process is about making you an engaged and critical worker and learner and questions are a key part of this.

But, now you have some answers – enough anyway to make a start with your work based learning. And the best way to start is by making a start! You won't know everything – even your tutors, contrary to what they may think, don't know everything (!) – but you should have enough answers to make a beginning. And you'll find that your learning efforts help you to find answers to lots of questions – some of which you won't yet have discovered.

Finally – good luck and good learning. See you at graduation!

CHAPTER ONE:

Value and Values

Why choose WBL?

Before starting a university-level WBL programme there are some important questions for you to ask and things to consider. In this chapter we will explore the value of a WBL approach and the values that lie within it, and see some real examples of others' experiences.

WBL is increasingly used as a mode of study for employed people and as a way of introducing change of practices within the workplace. It focuses on learning in and from the workplace where work, rather than a set curriculum, provides the focus for the learning programme. It promotes awareness of the workplace as a learning environment and uses this to extend the learner's capability and individual effectiveness.

It uses flexible approaches to learning that respond to the needs of the workplace and it enables individuals, groups of learners and employers to negotiate flexible and bespoke programmes of study through clear and robust processes.

What do we mean by WBL in higher education?

Higher education (HE), sometimes called university-level education, begins at the level immediately beyond the level of secondary education or NVQ level 3 and goes right through to doctoral (or PhD) level. Although in HE the levels and standards are the same in both traditional and WBL programmes, the processes are somewhat different. A WBL programme will not offer you a set syllabus, nor will you find a heavy attendance requirement at the university. Indeed in some WBL programmes learners may never physically attend the university. Much of the learning you do will be at your place of work. You will use your work situation as the focus for your study and you will negotiate your programme of learning with your university tutor and most likely your workplace. Often, learners gain considerable guidance and support from their tutor online.

At HE level, a WBL qualification is somewhat different to what you might initially understand as WBL. For example, HE WBL programmes are quite different from National Vocational Qualifications (NVQs), which ask you to demonstrate particular skills and knowledge assessed against occupational standards. Although at the start of an the programme you might match your development against occupational standards or your employers' needs, the main focus is the demonstration of your ability to reflect upon your skills, knowledge and approach to your work, often called your 'professional practice'. In some situations, learners will develop occupational competence *alongside* the WBL programme and this is usually assessed separately by the employer.

As a work based learner you will be expected to investigate a work based issue, which is likely to result in a real change of practice within your workplace. The extent and potential impact of this innovation will vary depending upon your individual role, your position within the organisation and the size and level of the project module undertaken.

WBL programmes are designed to promote professional and personal development and intended to benefit both learners and the workplace. Inter-personal, inter-professional, intellectual and practical skills are developed through each learner's recognition and reflection upon his or her professional development and the application of this to the workplace. A major aspect of work based programmes is the relationship between individual learning and organisational change.

Is it worth it?

As most university WBL qualifications can be customized to individual requirements, you will probably have the opportunity to negotiate the content, pace and mode of programme study. This flexibility within WBL means that your programme should be relevant to and manageable for both you and your employer. With this flexibility comes responsibility and, with guidance and support from your tutor, you as the learner will be responsible for ensuring that your WBL programme meets your skills and qualification needs and meets your employer's business needs and goals.

What is the status of a WBL qualification?

A higher education WBL qualification has the same status as any other higher education qualification. The main difference between a work based approach and traditional HE study is the *context* through which you will learn, meaning that you will focus on your role in the workplace, rather than on a text-based, pre-set syllabus. The title of a WBL qualification and the quality assurance procedures by which it is governed will be equal to other qualifications offered by the university.

Who else has done this kind of university qualification?

Work based learners come from a wide range of occupations and work at a variety of levels within their organisations. WBL qualifications are not just for managers or those in roles traditionally accepted to be 'professional' but are appropriate for everyone who is in either paid or voluntary work and capable of studying at a level within higher education.

WBL qualifications are designed for learners who demand:

- **flexibility** in their programmes of study;

- **formal recognition** for the level at which they are working in their occupational roles;

- **support** with their career development and progression.

Examples of a range of current work based learners' occupations, levels and motivations are:

- **a hairdresser** on a WBL business management programme. In order to enable him to start his own business, he needs to be able to identify the business needs of a salon and be able to study outside of his working hours;

- **an environmental health professional** wants to gain a postgraduate qualification that will meet her continuing professional development obligation to her professional body (the Chartered Institute of Environmental Health) through a workplace project;

- **a travel agent** identifies a significant increase in the number of clients making legal claims and identifies a professional development opportunity to gain a university qualification in the highly specialised field of package holiday law;

- **a fireman** wanting to improve his professional prospects is studying for a degree in public services management and requires a programme that allows him to reflect on his practice at work, whilst allowing him to manage his formal study time around his shifts at work;

- **a senior manager** in the retail business has few formally recognised qualifications but is 'qualified' to do her job through the experience she has acquired and the competence she demonstrates in the workplace. Both she and her employer want to see her level of work formally recognised through a qualification.

Such learners are people who often work full-time and require programmes that will offer them flexibility in:

- **delivery** – Work based learners are not usually people who can be available for on-campus classes five days a week. Flexible delivery can mean programmes offered by distance learning; online learning; weekend or evening classes; telephone and online support from tutors and other learners. Individuals do not necessarily have to work alone – a team approach is often encouraged, and quite often learners are able to meet to exchange views and ideas with other learners working on comparable projects;

- **duration and level** – A university programme could be as short as one term or semester in length, or could be a full degree programme lasting 3–5 years. It is dependent upon the needs of the learners and/or their employers;

- **progression opportunities** – WBL programmes should always include progression routes so that at the end of a programme the qualification gained should offer access onto either a larger programme, or a higher level of learning, thus allowing learners to progress in terms of both their qualifications and their professional profile;

- **content** – Content is not preset by the university, but agreed by negotiation between tutor and learner and sometimes with input from the employer or line manager. Different universities approach WBL in different ways, but they all stress the fact that you must play an active part in designing your programme and that there must be relevance to your work role. Most universities have flexible frameworks within which programmes are focused on the workplace and allow learners to concentrate on issues and projects at work that are directly applicable to their work-roles.

WBL is not an easy study option and as a successful learner you will have, or will develop, specific characteristics and skills that support your learning processes. As a work based learner you must be willing to assume responsibility for your own learning, as the nature of learning at or through work moves the focus of responsibility firmly into your hands. Individual learners take responsibility not only for identifying their learning needs and aspirations but also for managing the learning process. For a group of learners who share a single employer much of the identification of needs will be negotiated between the employer and university, although even in this context, individuals will negotiate their specific focus of learning, for example through identifying and developing their individual work based projects. So, to a greater or lesser extent, all work based learners negotiate their learning where the workplace provides the curriculum focus.

What experiences have the learners had?

Experiences of WBL can be widely varied, which is a result of the flexible nature of this type of study. Learners negotiate several aspects of their programmes and, as programmes are not class-room based, the individual learner also has a great deal of flexibility in deciding on how they want to manage their study time.

Paul is studying for a BA degree in Public Services Management based on his fire service career. Like many learners, he has found it difficult to balance his work, home and study commitments, especially with shift working patterns. However, he has appreciated the support he receives from both his manager at work and his tutors while studying. As his studies are based on his place of work, he feels that he hasn't had to segregate his studies from his work. Much of the project investigation he has carried out for his studies are part of his regular responsibilities at work.

'I believe that his module has started me thinking in a more strategic manner, given me the confidence to challenge the accepted way of approaching things and made me realise that I have important contributions to make.'

Jamal has been studying for an MA Professional Practice (Education Leadership). He valued the phased approach of his learning programme, which introduced theories and current thinking about his professional work before he was required to start his own investigations and project. This approach meant that he could recognise where theory was applied to practice and begin to understand the influences of national policy on his own work. He negotiated his work based investigation and final report with his tutors and his line manager, which gave him a sense of being in control of the pace and level of his learning. He thoroughly enjoyed the practical nature of his project as it was relevant to his role, appropriate to his workload and brought him into contact with contemporaries in the workplace and other work based learners at the university.

'The experiential nature of this course matches the way I learn best. I find I can understand information more effectively if I can relate it to my own experience, practice and purposes. I feel that I will get more out of the course because I will be building my own programme, choosing the project, materials, objectives. It suits my personal style of learning.'

An unexpected benefit of carrying out his project was that as his profile at work was raised he was perceived as being the expert in his field.

CASE STUDY

Claire, an environmental health officer working for a city council, appreciated the flexibility of her learning programme. She experienced some unanticipated changes to her domestic situation and thought at one point that she would be unable to complete her studies. However, with the support of her employer and guidance from her tutors, she was able to adjust her work and study pattern and found that in needing to renegotiate her work and study times she was by no means unusual. She decided the best approach would be to allocate a regular time for her studies, which would take place on the university campus so she could use the facilities there and remain free from interruptions.

Whilst Claire said that juggling work, study and family had not been an easy task, she reported that organising the division between work and study helped her thinking processes and to visualise more clearly how her organisation works. The new routine suited her well and she believes her studies have put her in a better position to make a meaningful contribution to her organisation. Claire plans to build on her current programme of study by moving on to a master's degree.

Louise, a linen supervisor for a hospital trust, became interested in infection control in hospitals. She observed that her work based study:

'...offered me flexibility and it gave me the opportunity to take stock of what I had been doing on a regular basis.'

Through the module she sought to investigate the policies, procedures and evidence for the storage and transportation of linen around the hospital. She researched soft furnishings and fabrics that can reduce cross infection and she is currently helping to update trust policy. Her proposals were considered by the senior management group and the trust invested a significant sum to implement her recommendations. Louise received a Regional Adult Learners Award from the National Institute for Advancement in Continuing Education (NIACE).

These work based learners' experiences show that an organised approach to study is a necessity. University tutors who support work based learners understand the demands and rigour of working and studying concurrently and provide support to learners in developing their time management and other study skills. Many learners are also supported by a workplace advisor or mentor but, even in circumstances where this may not be possible, learners are likely to find themselves part of a cohort of learners with similar experiences and demands on their time. Repeatedly, learners recount their learning experiences as very positive in terms of their own personal growth, their professional development and emerging opportunities.

What are the likely benefits and drawbacks for me?

The value you get from your programme will, like most things in life, be based upon the levels of commitment energy you are able to put into it.

Regardless of your role in the workplace, through your programme of study you should learn how to evaluate work processes and to identify opportunities for improvement. Through receiving feedback from peers and university tutors you will learn how to see criticism as a tool with which you can improve your studies and your practice at work. These high level skills should help increase your confidence, both in your studies and through applying new-found knowledge in the workplace.

Formally recognised WBL qualifications support career development and progression. Individuals do not necessarily have to work alone as a team approach is often acceptable, and quite often learners are able to meet to exchange views and ideas with other learners working on comparable projects.

Learners report that their level of performance at work and their standing in the workplace improves during and after their WBL programme. As a work based learner, you will undoubtedly gain a greater insight and understanding of your organisation, and your programme of study may lead to improved and new relationships within and across organisations, as you take up opportunities to compare practice with fellow learners.

More and more universities are recognising the value of offering WBL programmes which enable learners to achieve nationally recognised qualifications. Workers within specialist fields often find that to increase their professional standing they need to demonstrate continuing professional development to the professional or industry body which represents their area of work. Many of these professional bodies work in partnership with universities to ensure that the WBL programmes are appropriate to the needs of the sector. In some professional fields, WBL qualifications may be used to meet the professional body's CPD requirements. This means that learners can meet the needs of their professional body whilst simultaneously achieving a nationally recognised university qualification.

WBL is not without drawbacks of course. As previously discussed, a sound approach to managing competing demands on your time is essential. It can also be difficult to remain focused on specific work projects or issues if changes in employment are pending or planned. Managing the transition between changing work environments as a result of employment or organisational changes can create its own challenges. However, these should be viewed as challenges rather than barriers, and your tutor should understand the inevitability of these situations and offer you support at such times.

Many tutors of WBL report that some learners become so engrossed in the subject of their studies that they could exceed the requirements of the programme by a large margin. In some cases learners have developed to an extent where they have, in effect, outgrown the responsibilities and challenges of their existing work role. It is not unusual for learners studying at HE level to seek increased responsibility and opportunities, to put newfound skills into practice within their professional role, to gain a promotion, or even to change job. This demonstrates the positive impact and value that study can have for a learner.

In summary, people in work are increasingly undertaking WBL qualifications because they:

- are able to see direct relevance between studying for a qualification through WBL and their role in the workplace;
- can obtain support from their employers;
- are able to develop the programme around their own professional development needs and individual interests;
- are able to negotiate the focus, context, timescale and assessment of their work;
- can fit this flexible form of study into their working and personal lives;
- view studying for an accredited qualification as evidence of commitment to their professional role;
- seek career progression and the potential for increased earnings.

What are the likely benefits and drawbacks for my employer?

The government is committed to encouraging employers and universities to work together in order to develop more flexible ways of learning to meet economic and workforce development needs. There are indications that businesses that engage and invest in training are stronger and more successful organisations than those which ignore the training and development needs of their employees.

Whether because of governmental initiatives or independent of them, employers are increasingly approaching universities to develop WBL programmes for their staff. The value for them is that:

- staff undertake real-work projects which offer direct benefit to their organisation;

- the workforce becomes motivated and focused on organisational challenges;

- staff on WBL programmes become more closely engaged in organisational processes;

- increased loyalty results from the visible and tangible investment in the development of the workforce;

- staff retention rates are improved, and the enhanced capabilities of the existing workforce can help with recruitment – both as a means of attracting new employees, but also as a means of promoting from within the organisation;

- studying on a WBL programme can help employees to achieve their full potential;

- they can work with a university to develop a programme which not only supports the professional development of their staff but which also focuses on organisational improvement;

- organisational and culture change can be effected through small scale developments via WBL projects;

- WBL can be a means of addressing and meeting an organisation's business plans.

Supporting staff in their professional development is not without challenges for employers. Some employers are cautious in supporting professional development in their workforce, arguing that newly qualified employees will want to move to another employer. Whilst this is always a possibility, motivated and ambitious employees will usually view an employer willing to invest in their staff's professional development in a positive light and employees are more likely to remain loyal to them, knowing that they have that support in place. Employers who invest in their workforce rarely have difficulty in recruiting high quality staff.

Some employers are prepared to pay the programme tuition fees on behalf of their employees or enter into a partial-payment arrangement with them. Others may choose to offer their support in kind, such as study leave, offering the support of a workplace mentor, use of a computer, or a quiet space to study. Some employers have found that paying tuition fees for their employees' university-level WBL programmes works out cheaper than buying in staff training. Each organisation is unique and has its own approach to staff development, so you should talk with your line manager to find out what could be available to you.

What do employers think about university-level WBL qualifications?

CASE STUDY

A healthcare NHS foundation trust has made a significant investment in their workforce by offering a Professional Practice Programme in collaboration with a university. This has enabled the development of new models for delivery of learning which match the needs of staff, accommodating shift and rota patterns of working. Terry, a workforce development manager, states:

'We have found the programme to be a fantastic opportunity for colleagues, giving us a chance to better ourselves, and work towards futures with improved prospects.'

CASE STUDY

A large national building organisation, comprising a number of companies operating in the engineering, construction and services sector, has also worked with a university to offer high-level workforce development via WBL. As a result of the impact that the learners have had on the business, the organisation has come to recognise the potential for more extensive industry-wide links.

CASE STUDY

Due to new legislation, non-law firms can now offer legal advice to the public. One such organisation recognised the value of accredited specialised training programmes for their staff, with a direct benefit to the organisation in having recognised training for practitioners, which is hard to obtain outside a traditional law practice. The learning programmes developed in collaboration with a university have been an effective and positive way to motivate the organisation's staff and have met their workforce development needs within their own work environment.

Is it easy or is it really difficult?

The academic rigour of your qualification will be of the same standard as comparable taught university qualifications, but WBL will make different demands on you. You may be feeling apprehensive about either studying at, or returning to study at university. Priorities and challenges will be different for each individual but the following are all worth consideration:

Practicalities to consider

- Work/family commitments and pressures can generate many issues for work based learners;

- It is important to engage your employer's or line manager's support as soon as possible. They may be able to offer financial help, study leave or other forms of support;

- Much WBL is supported online, so you will need to ensure that you have access to IT resources. This might be via your workplace, university, library or home.

Personal skills and characteristics

- Much of the control and responsibility for the learning lies with the learner rather than with the tutor. This requires significant individual commitment from you;

- There is considerable freedom, but this brings the expectation that you will be willing and able to self-direct your study;

- IT skills: most work based learners are expected to access their learning materials, communicate with their tutor and other learners and conduct research and other information searches online. Many universities will deliver their programmes through an online 'learning platform' such as Blackboard or WebCT as well as using social networking systems such as blogs and wikis. However, most institutions will offer introductory support whilst learners familiarise themselves with the university environment and IT platforms.

Academic and learning style issues

Many learners may be initially concerned about the assessment process. This is understandable, particularly for those who have been away from formal learning for some time. However, most tutors are aware of this and are generally very supportive in giving clear assignment information and helpful feedback on your work.

WBL requires self-directed learning. The role of the WBL tutor is to facilitate your learning, but you will manage both the content and processes of your programme of learning. You will be encouraged to pursue your own lines of enquiry and engage with your workplace in ways that may be outside the normal practice of your work routine. Managing the pace and direction of the learning rests mostly with you and, initially, you may find this difficult to grasp or feel comfortable with. Similarly, you need to become conscious of your own learning patterns and feel confident in consulting your tutor for advice.

For some there is a danger of becoming so closely absorbed in their work project that they lose sight of the whole learning cycle and become unable, at least temporarily, to disengage from the work project itself and thus are not able to review their learning progress. The ability to stand back from situations and be able to think critically and reflectively is a key skill, which you will develop under the guidance and support of your tutor and with peers.

It becomes evident that WBL does not offer an easy route. What it does offer though is the prospect of rewarding intellectual challenge and opportunities for professional and personal growth.

What will I get at the end of it?

Successful graduates benefit from the formal acknowledgement of their professional performance. Many work based learners start their university study with no formal qualifications beyond secondary education, yet they work successfully in jobs that demand a much higher level of knowledge and skill than their qualifications reflect. Enrolment on a work based qualification allows you to study at a level that reflects the level of your current working practice. This formal acknowledgement of your professional capabilities can be hugely rewarding.

Work based learning has the potential to make changes in the workplace.

You will find that studying for a qualification in this way gives you the time, focus and support to reflect on how you perform at work, how the workplace operates, what beneficial changes can be made and how you can work effectively towards implementing those changes.

Although rewarding, working and studying concurrently is not an easy option and most work based learners report a huge sense of personal achievement in juggling these demands, along with their family and personal lives. Most universities will offer support in developing time management and study skills. However, there is no magic fix for this challenge. It demands commitment, focus and hard work.

Skills and knowledge

At the beginning of a WBL programme, you will probably undertake an exercise through which you will identify the skills and knowledge you already have. The result of this exercise is often a pleasant surprise for learners as, given time to reflect, they often identify things that they had overlooked or taken for granted. This exercise may partially determine the level of your programme and the skills and knowledge you will be expected to acquire throughout your programme.

It is likely that your programme will be made up of a number of related modules. Embedded in each module will be a collection or list of learning outcomes that you must meet in order to pass. Ultimately, you will be awarded a qualification once your university agrees that you have reached the required level of learning through having achieved the learning outcomes. Below is an example of the learning outcomes from a typical WBL module entitled, Work Based Project.

Work Based Project Module

In this module, learners are required to identify a work based project that provides the opportunity for personal, professional and organisational development. The learner will accept responsibility for developing and managing this project.

Learning outcomes

Upon successful completion of this module the learner will be able to:

- identify and negotiate a project that addresses issues relevant to the learner's personal goals and immediate area of responsibility within the workplace;

- select and use appropriate skills and techniques to carry out small-scale practical investigations which will include addressing relevant ethical, commercial, confidential and data protection issues;

- use prior knowledge, new learning and a range of specialised skills to tackle relevant issues;

- consider a variety of courses of actions and make decisions based on informed judgments;

- use appropriate theories, frameworks and principles relevant to the issues/situations addressed in the project;

- plan and manage a project within an agreed framework;

- present the project demonstrating presentational and report writing skills;

- make recommendations that will impact upon the learner's own work role and immediate working environment.

The learning outcomes above are 'core' learning outcomes. This means that every person taking this module, regardless of their professional role or the sector in which they work, will work towards achieving them. However, as mentioned earlier in this chapter, you will be expected to negotiate some of the content of your programme. At this stage you may develop, in negotiation with your tutor and line manager or employer, further learning outcomes to be incorporated into your programme specific to your learning and work context.

Qualifications

The qualification you obtain will be dependent upon on the level of your study and whether you undertake a full academic programme, such as an honours degree (undergraduate) or a master's degree (postgraduate); a staged programme (a qualification which comprises part of a full degree) such as a certificate, advanced diploma or postgraduate certificate or undertake a module or modules of a degree. The table on page 20 offers a structure of qualifications offered by most universities. However, this is not definitive and you may find different universities offer qualifications that are not included in this table.

Initially, you may choose to register just for one or two modules that may not be sufficient to constitute a qualification but to which you can add subsequent modules at a later date in order to achieve a qualification. Whether you undertake a large or smaller programme of study, the qualification is equivalent to similar university qualifications studied in a more traditional manner. If you successfully complete a degree or staged (interim) qualification you will receive a certificate from the university in which you enrolled, and you will be entitled to attend the graduation ceremony and use the appropriate letters after your name.

Professional qualifications

People sometimes expect that they can become a nurse, social worker, or similar professional, by successful completion of a WBL programme. This is not so. Professional qualifications are protected by strict rules concerning the balance between theory and supervised practice, and the content of professional education and training is very carefully controlled to ensure consistency between difference educational providers. This is not what WBL, as defined in this book, is about.

Professional recognition

Many people, such as teachers, engineers, environmental scientists, to name but a few, are bound by their profession to evidence their engagement with some form of continuing professional development

(CPD). Although a WBL university qualification is an academic qualification and not a professional qualification, WBL qualifications are often recognised by professional bodies as meeting professional CPD requirements. Many universities offer qualification titles that reflect the nature of the programme, such as a *BA (Hons) International Business Practice* and *MA Professional Practice (Education)*.

Progression to further qualifications

Most WBL programmes will be part of a progression route so that through further study you can progress to higher level qualifications within your sector or profession. Some universities offer a work based route from entry at undergraduate level all the way through to a professional doctorate. Once you have attained a work based qualification or even modules of a programme at one particular university, it is very possible that you could use these to progress onto a programme at another university that recognises your qualification. Acceptance onto the new programme will be dependent upon the entry regulations of that particular university and the programme entry requirements.

What do we mean by employer, employment and learner?

Employer

Within the context of WBL the term 'employer' can be understood and defined in several ways. Your employer can be either a business or person for whom you work. However, the definition may also extend to include your employer's representative, which could mean your line manager or other more senior colleague.

If, like many people, you are self-employed you take on the mantle of employer as well as that of learner. There are many such people who enrol on WBL programmes. In this situation it is likely that you too will need someone to provide you with support from the workplace. In the absence of an employer or line manager, you might elect to find yourself a mentor (someone working at a similar or higher level and who is not unfamiliar with your sector or business), with whom you can discuss workplace ideas. Such people are often flattered by such a request, and provide invaluable support.

Employment

To be eligible for study in a WBL programme you must be actively engaged in work, which is defined as a 'purposeful activity' whether paid or on a voluntary basis. This is because the central methodology of WBL is to learn to improve your practice in the workplace, through drawing on real work situations. The term 'employment' covers a range of situations including:

- paid work;
- unpaid work, which could include voluntary work or working within a family business without receiving remuneration;
- full-time or part-time employment;
- self-employed workers and business owners – from actors, artists and builders to farmers, gardeners and restaurateurs.

In short, WBL is for anyone who is regularly engaged in work, (or undertakes periods of contractual work sufficiently long enough to complete the programme of study) whatever the nature of that work.

Learner

You will find the term 'learner' rather than 'student' is generally used for those who study through WBL. Firstly, the term 'student' tends to imply that person's primary role is to study, whereas work based learners already have a key identity through their role at work. Secondly, we tend to think of being a student as a role that has a relatively short shelf life, whereas through WBL you will be encouraged to become a learner who continues to learn throughout your professional life, beyond the duration of your formal programme of study.

University Qualifications

Credit Level	University Award	Award Titles and Abbreviations	Credit Requirement
UNDERGRADUATE			
Level 4 *	Certificate	U Cert	60 credits at level 4
Level 4	Certificate of Higher Education	Cert HE	120 credits at level 4
Level 5	Diploma	U Dip	60 credits at level 5
Level 5	Diploma of Higher Education	Dip HE	240 credits; 120 at level 4, 120 at level 5
Level 5	Foundation Degree	Fd	240 credits; 120 at level 4, 120 at level 5
Level 6	Advanced Diploma	Adv Dip	60 credits at level 6
Level 6	Advanced Diploma of Higher Education	Adv Dip HE	300 credits; 120 at level 4, 120 at level 5, 60 at level 6
Level 6	Ordinary Degree	Bachelor of Arts (BA) Bachelor of Science (BSc)	300 credits; 120 at level 4, 120 at level 5, 60 at level 6
Level 6	Honours Degree	Bachelor of Arts (Hons) Bachelor of Science (Hons)	360 credits; 120 at level 4, 120 at level 5, 120 at level 6
POSTGRADUATE (can include up to 20 credits at level 6)			
Level 7	Postgraduate Certificate	PG Cert	60 credits at level 7
Level 7	Postgraduate Diploma	PG Dip	120 credits at level 7
Level 7	Master's Degree	Master of Arts (MA) Master of Science (MSc) Master of Business Administration (MBA) Master of Education (MEd)	180 credits at level 7
Level 8	Professional Doctorate	Doctor of Philosophy (PhD) Doctor of Professional Studies (DProf)	540 credits; maximum 180 at level 7, minimum 360 at level 8

*Level 4 corresponds to the first year of an undergraduate degree programme

CHAPTER TWO

Work Based Learning: the Big Idea

Now you've heard something about WBL programmes, it's probably time to step back a little and find out something of what the thinking is behind WBL at university level. The big idea in the shortest chapter!

What are the principles of WBL in higher education?

If the big idea is to recognise higher learning wherever it has taken place and reward those who have achieved it with university qualifications, then a key principle of WBL in higher education is capturing and recognising informal learning.

We know that high-level learning doesn't just take place in 'formal' lecture theatres, classrooms and laboratories on university campuses, but goes on in many other locations too. All the time, people at work do complex tasks. They solve problems. They apply their knowledge gained from past experience to new situations. They might think of new and better ways to do the job. They may work alone. They may share their knowledge with others. They may learn from others. And all the time, as people work to achieve what their job requires, they are using and developing their understanding. In other words, they are learning.

Work based learning is useful because the skills people develop at work help them to solve familiar problems. Of course, some work based problems will be unfamiliar and people will deal with the new situation and solve the problem by applying the skills and knowledge they have learned previously. Knowledge and skills learned in the workplace keep businesses and organisations going. They are also the levers for developing and moving these businesses and organisations forward.

Most of the time, this useful workplace learning is informal. Further, as well as being informal, it might be described as tacit, that is, understood and recognised without being stated explicitly. Even this tacit awareness might not involve many people – maybe just those in the workplace who are directly involved, perhaps only one person – the one doing the learning. Companies and organisations will contain lots of people with skills and knowledge, but are unlikely to know all the things that all their employees know. WBL can, by capturing and articulating the informal, really provide benefits for companies in knowing what they are good at and where there are opportunities for development.

Work based learning in higher education focuses attention on the informal learning that develops through the process of doing work. It seeks to make the learning explicit, to make it planned rather than incidental and to present this planned, explicit higher level learning in a way that allows it to be recognised at university level and, in doing so, it benefits both the learners and their organisations.

Within universities offering WBL programmes, there is also an understanding that work based learners who focus their studies on work activities are unlikely to be starting from square one in terms of their higher level understanding of their work. So, WBL seeks to recognise what skills, knowledge and understanding work based learners bring to their studies. This is called Accreditation of Prior Experiential Learning (APEL). APEL helps learners to present learning which has previously been unrecognised and perhaps unseen and to map this against the criteria for university-level qualifications. Learners are encouraged to think about what they have already learnt and which they can bring to the start of their study. The recognition and accreditation of prior experiential learning puts an academic value, not on experience, but on *learning* from experience, and is an important part of capturing the informal.

Another key principle of WBL is to give learners and their company or organisation a say in what they decide to learn, how they go about learning and how they will show what they have learned. Rather than having a set content like a traditional university programme, WBL looks to take work activities and professional practice as the starting point to build a university-level curriculum which is personally and professionally relevant. The idea is to have learners actively involved in planning, managing and driving forward their own learning, rather than being the passive recipients of parcels of knowledge which are 'delivered' to them.

What does it mean to be a work based learner in higher education?

If you have made the decision to engage in university level WBL you'll have a keen sense of yourself in your professional location. Many WBL learners have skills, expertise and status in the workplace that goes far beyond their paper qualifications. Often, they are looking to their studies to enhance work based abilities or provide credentials by achieving a university level qualification.

Learners come to WBL with a variety of different motivations. For example

> **CASE STUDY**
>
> Derek is a designer and was seeking:
>
> '...an increased level of academic knowledge in combination with my practical work experience to give more context to my work and enable me to talk more confidently about my area of expertise.'

> **CASE STUDY**
>
> Sarah is in marketing and:
>
> '...hoped to learn new methods of planning and setting goals, I was keen to adapt new ideas into my job and to have the 25 years I have spent within business validated so that I can comfortably share my skills with those at the beginning of their careers.'

CASE STUDY

Diane is a manager:

'the combination of work focus and academic rigour in a programme of study was beyond my expectations. I wouldn't have read about things without this course. It has given me an understanding of the background and it has all been terribly relevant. Everything I learn I use. Currently, every proactive decision I make for the business is a result of research from my studies.'

CASE STUDY

Being a work based learner in higher education has, for many learners, really helped their companies. Julie works in retail:

'My programme has created a lot of conversations within the business that we wouldn't have had. I am constantly looking at ways to diversify. It has helped me hugely. Without the course I would have gone on as before. I am convinced that my studies have helped the business in which I work to be sleeker and more professional and, most importantly... remain profitable.'

What are the differences and similarities between WBL and traditional higher education?

If your university-level WBL programme is to mean anything, then it must be clearly recognisable as higher education. It must be just as challenging as more traditional university study. In the UK, this means that, like all other university programmes, your study is mapped against the Level Descriptors in the Framework for Higher Education Qualifications (FHEQ) – essentially the output statements for university qualifications. This is *very* important and it guarantees your WBL programme is really *higher* education.

By ensuring that WBL programmes align with this framework, universities are able to offer the flexibility for learners and their companies to shape and make a qualification of personal and professional relevance, based on a curriculum of work and accessed in a way which is personally and professionally appropriate and to make sure that such qualifications meet clearly identified higher education standards.

University-level WBL is judged by the same standards as other university-level learning so you'll be expected to show the same qualities and attributes as other learners in higher education and to develop the same higher level skills. These might be seen as developing knowledge and understandings of a field or fields of study and being able to apply these understandings in a range of situations. You'll also be expected to show the ability to solve problems, to make decisions, to analyse and evaluate and to be able to communicate all these qualities to others. The difference is that, in WBL, the focus is on the many different kinds of knowledge used at work, rather than on a single subject.

Isn't WBL just the same as NVQ?

National Vocational Qualifications (NVQs) have been around for more than 20 years now. They are work related and are based on the skills and knowledge needed to do a job. They might be termed 'competence-based' as they describe what competent people in a particular occupation are expected to be able to do. WBL in higher education differs from NVQs as it looks to reflect the capability of skilled people in the workplace to handle the unfamiliar and unexpected.

University-level WBL is about learning, not training. This means that, like all successful HE learners, you will need to move towards becoming an independent learner, capable of critical and reflective thinking, with the ability to apply what you've learned in different situations. Your study will combine academic and theoretical knowledge with work based skills with the aim of satisfying both academic and professional requirements.

Approaches to Learning

What is really exciting about university-level WBL is that you can align what you are doing at work with what you are learning, and vice versa.

This chapter will explore in more detail what you will learn, and how you can build upon your existing learning from experience in work and in wider aspects of your life, through processes called accreditation of prior experiential learning (APEL). It will also explain how your learning will be assessed, and introduce the concept of learning outcomes which are key to success in higher education, particularly in negotiated WBL. The achievement of clearly specified learning outcomes is central to assessment processes by which you will gain credits towards your eventual qualification.

All negotiated WBL programmes place considerable emphasis upon adult learners being independent learners, critical thinkers, and reflective practitioners, so these ideas are explored to help you identify your own reaction to these principles.

Throughout the chapter the role of tutors is also mentioned, and the potential for contact with others at work, in networks, or with other learners on similar programmes. There are also examples of what real people have done, to help you think about how WBL might work for you.

How will I start?

Obviously programmes across different universities will differ, but most work based learning programmes have a strong and often early emphasis on exploring your own situation. They encourage you to think in some detail across a broad range of issues beyond what you may have put into your application to study at university level.

This initial process of reflection can be given different titles. Sometimes, for example, it may be called Personal Development Planning (PDP). In other situations, it may form part of negotiating a learning agreement, plan or contract, in sections which cover your existing experience and qualifications, and in which you respond to questions about your current situation and the challenges you face.

This kind of reflection on your own development is already built into many workplaces or professions, and many of you will recognise that you are involved in it through processes of induction, appraisal and professional development.

Considering what you have already learnt may prompt discussions with your tutor about claiming credit for learning you have already achieved. This may be for formal courses and training at an appropriate level (APL) or it may be for informal learning you have achieved at work (APEL). In thinking about APEL, start by asking yourself: 'What do I already know that I can build upon?'

When you have identified some learning you've achieved, the next questions to ask yourself would be:

- Is it up to date?

- Is it relevant to the aims of my study?

- Is it higher level learning?

- Can I provide evidence?

Many learners find it gives them a sense of real pride in previous achievements to have this recognised as worthy of university-level credits. Gaining recognition for your prior learning may also be a very practical help in keeping costs of fees lower, and helping you to accumulate credits more quickly. The prospect of saving both money and time can really help your motivation too!

You will usually have good tutorial support throughout such early processes, as it helps your tutor to really feel they are getting to know you too even if you are working at a distance from your chosen university and you never, or seldom, meet face to face. Tutors want to be able to help you as effectively as possible, and they recognise that positive relationships need to be established early on. It is really important to use your tutor effectively, asking focused questions, especially when you first start. You will probably need less support once you are fully involved in your learning and feel more confident through feedback on your progress. Having said that, do try to help yourself too by finding answers to questions in various ways, for example through student forums (often online), frequently asked questions, help and support documents, websites and books.

How will I learn?

Different WBL programmes offer different blends of learning and modes of study, ranging from taught-on-campus modules, through the use of e-learning modules to university-level study based around projects, issues and skill development tailored to workplace needs.

It is a good idea at an early stage to write down ideas about how you can plan your study time to suit your own situation. Planning your time can help you to see where compromise might be needed, especially when juggling a range of demands like family commitments. What can you realistically fit in and at what pace might you be able to study? Another significant question can be to ask how you learn best. For example, can you study independently, setting and maintaining your own patterns of work and keeping to deadlines? Or do you need to learn alongside others, or in ways that are already structured by teaching materials?

CASE STUDY

Michael owns and runs a successful hairdressing salon:

'Wherever there's a PC, you can study.'

Robert is a production worker:

'Rather than fitting around work, I found that I made use of those wasted times you don't think you can do anything with. I remember once taking my car for a service, thinking about the 101 things I could be doing instead of sitting around bored. I spied a computer in the waiting room and ended up doing some work on marketing right there in the garage!'

Susan is a teaching assistant in a secondary school:

'If I had any problems I could email my tutors for advice, assistance and encouragement, which was a great help whilst dealing with my hectic family life.'

What will I learn?

Your work situation will provide a rich source of work projects, which you can undertake more effectively by combining them with study.

Specific questions to ask when identifying such learning opportunities might include:

- What does my employer want me to do?

- What do I need to know or be able to do to get to my next grade or promotion?

- What objectives have been set in my annual review that I can use as a vehicle for higher learning?

- Does my professional body have any standards that I might be able to link to my studies?

Negotiated WBL in university-level programmes of study

One of the exciting and interesting opportunities that negotiated WBL offers is the ability to integrate real work projects and activities into your programme of study. The following learners offer examples of some possibilities.

CASE STUDY

Karen, a nurse:

'I would have had to do this project for work anyway, but as I was also doing it for my studies I delved into it more and did it better and came out with something more satisfying to me and with more influence and impact at work. So it's taking my job, which is what I think is important, and getting a lot more background development and knowledge to take my job further, as well as getting a qualification.'

CASE STUDY

Michael, owner/ manager of a hairdressing salon:

'We're working smarter now. My new marketing plans mean we're drawing in more of the type of work we're good at – making more money for working less! I now know how to recruit staff due to my Human Resources Management module. And the shop is a happier place, because we've hired staff who want what we offer as an employer. When I have time off now, I have peace of mind because the team have the policies and procedures I drew upon within the course to fall back on.'

CASE STUDY

Shirley is deputy manager of a retail pharmacy:

'Your studies relate to your work and provide you and your employer with tangible results as you proceed... the content arises directly from the work I do and directly feeds back into it. Currently, every proactive decision I make for the business is a result of research that is being used in my studies.'

Here is a non-exclusive list of some of the kinds of assignments or projects undertaken at work by learners engaged in university-level WBL. You won't either want or be able to attempt them all, but some of them may appeal to you or perhaps spark off your own ideas to develop for study.

Examples of typical WBL assignments

- involvement in strategic/product development

- designing something new and justifying it

- reporting on developing and managing systems, services, and/ or functions

- writing for or presenting at professional/occupational conferences

- research or investigation relating to your work activities or processes

- reading about and reporting on your technical field, business and/or management practices for identified audiences in your organisation

Below are some more detailed examples of how learners have built specific modules of study relating to issues and concerns in their workplaces.

Examples of learner-specific modules of study

- a module focused on the analysis of company policies, particularly in relation to health and safety, risk assessment and contracts of employment

- a module focusing on organisational strategies and tools to stimulate innovation and creativity to develop profitability

- a module concerned with leading and managing people in a changing environment and focused on formulating a management approach appropriate to the workplace, based on theories of good practice in leadership

- a project focused on selecting appropriate tools for a team within the organisation, and evaluating the application of learning to the cycles of project management

- a project focused on understanding equality and diversity principles and concepts in order to develop a training manual to train trainers on human rights laws

- a project focused on developing ballet teaching techniques

While you may be clear about work projects or activities you want to include in your higher education programme, it's important to ensure that the learning outcomes from your work and the products and evidence of your learning are presented in a format that is suitable for accreditation in higher education. You do not get credit simply for going to work! WBL also involves:

- adequate and appropriate research or inquiry;

- exploring beyond the immediate workplace and the points of view within it;

- networking with others working in the same field at the same or higher levels;

- exposure to intellectual challenge by tutors with relevant expertise and (where possible) professionals in appropriate fields of work;

- evaluation and reflection on progress with your learning and associated work processes.

University-level learning is based on the achievement of learning outcomes. While different universities offering WBL programmes will have different approaches, all modules and programmes will have learning outcomes in some form and in order to pass, you need to have achieved them.

Learning outcomes are statements of what it is expected that you will be able to do as a result of your learning activities. They will be related to the acquisition and demonstration of knowledge, understanding and intellectual and/or practical skills. Their purpose is to help you to sharpen the focus of your project or module, to identify its scope and boundaries and to provide a clear basis for planning your learning activities and their assessment. If appropriate, they can also be shared with workplace colleagues and/or mentors.

On some WBL programmes, learners develop and negotiate their own learning outcomes. Negotiated learning outcomes identify clear, mutually understood requirements for you and your tutor expressed as formal statements. These formal learning outcome statements describe the learning that you will have achieved on successful completion of a module and they form the basis for learning and assessment. Each learning outcome statement should describe a learning achievement which is considered fundamental to the purpose of the module. One of the fundamental issues is achieving the right balance between being too specific and too broad. When formulating learning outcomes, it helps to ask yourself: *'How will I demonstrate for assessment that I have achieved the learning intended in each one? What evidence will be most appropriate to present?'*

Your tutor will be a useful sounding board and will give you feedback as you formulate your learning outcomes, helping you to clarify them for a range of audiences and to shape the boundaries of your learning in a particular module.

Other universities have general or 'generic' learning outcomes for the programme as a whole that learners address through their work based assignments and projects.

What are the ethical issues and principles in WBL?

There are some important ethical issues for the work based learner to consider, and principles to apply, when undertaking WBL. Unlike campus-based students, the ethical issues are likely to be more complex, and more significant because the work based learner operates within workplace, occupational and sometimes professional contexts. These tend to add complexity compared with standard university education.

Being a worker–researcher / insider–researcher

Compared with a campus-based student, you are likely to have access to a range of confidential and sensitive information at work. This means that the information and knowledge you have of your specific workplace or area of professional practice needs to be handled more carefully than you would normally expect if, for example, you were simply writing an essay as part of a campus-based course. The work or professional context gives you special access to information, documents and 'insider' knowledge that needs to be handled in a careful way.

You are also likely to be working with other people in a set of complicated relationships. These might include work colleagues, managers, people you manage, as well as the clients or customers of your employer. You may also be working in a context where regulations or guidelines require you to work in particular ways.

The complexity of your work situation, and the special access you have to information and insider-knowledge means that as a learner, you need to ensure you consider and adopt the appropriate ethical approach to the way you conduct yourself. This is important because, as a learner, you will be sharing thoughts and writing about your work with others (tutors, other learners, people reading your project reports).

There are two main considerations. Firstly, any specific study assignment like a project will need to be carefully considered for any ethical concerns as part of its design. Secondly, you will need to think about the overall ethical implications of being a work based learner. Each university-level WBL programme will have its own ways of helping you think through the issues and will provide resources, guidebooks and other resources that you can use to help you understand the issues.

Peter works for an international commercial bank. He is Head of Computing Services. As a senior manger, he has access to a range of commercially and personally sensitive information, including information on the people working in his department. Peter is doing a work based postgraduate degree to help him redesign the regular reporting of financial information within the bank. Peter thinks the current systems don't work well and waste the bank a lot of money through inefficiency. However he is aware that redesigning the systems may possibly result in a reduction in staffing requirements. What he plans will not be popular with many people in his own department. He undertakes a 'Stakeholder Mapping' exercise to explore the likely consequences of his overall plans. This helps him realise the full implications to a range of stakeholders and suggests ways of dealing ethically with the issues. He proceeds with the project having considered that the interests of shareholders outweigh those of the implicated employees especially as the Director of Human Resources has indicated that most individuals would find equivalent work in other parts of the bank. Peter is acting ethically, because he is balancing the 'interests' of stakeholders (employees and shareholders) and using this process to limit the damage to his colleagues while meeting his responsibilities as a manager. When he realises the possible implications, he makes the effort to see how his organisation can limit the damage to the individuals by discussing it with the Head of Human Resources.

Ethical principles in WBL

We do not have established ways in which ethics within WBL are understood at a national level. Each university has its own ethical systems and procedures. However, there are several generally established ethical principles that you might consider as a work based learner.

Rights of others and the balancing of 'interests'

Everyone has rights and responsibilities (as a worker, as a citizen, a parent, a customer etc.). Acting ethically is the balancing of these in practice.

The professional context

If you are a specialist in an area of professional work, the ethical guidelines from that professional area will be very important in your work based studies. Generally, it is the professional guidelines and standards that will apply in your WBL activities. So for example, if you are working as a health professional, it is very likely that the university will ask for your project to pass through an Ethics Committee. If you are a school teacher, your head teacher should ask you to conform to established guidelines for research in an educational setting. Your university will be able to direct you to the appropriate guidelines in your subject or professional area of work.

Honesty and deception

The issue here is not just about acting dishonestly which is clearly wrong, but the subtle ways that we might represent ourselves and our actions in order to get someone's agreement or approval. It is easy to persuade ourselves that 'it's OK' to do something so we can access some information or to do something, which may be more deceptive than we intend. This includes representing the ideas, words and intellectual property of others properly in your work (see section on Plagiarism). Acting ethically means thinking carefully about our real intentions and not providing ourselves with easy excuses.

Sensitivity

Acting sensitively means that even while we act honestly and in a balanced way, we need to consider how other people might react. It's easy to offend unintentionally, and acting ethically is to think, before we act or speak, about how we might offend by our actions or words.

Confidentiality

All ethical guidelines will place confidentiality as an important issue to be considered. Confidentiality means protecting the identities of individuals or groups. This is particularly important where you are representing their critical viewpoints, where information about your informants should not be put into the public domain or where the subjects cannot exercise any control over you and your activities (e.g. a school student who participates in a project run by a teacher).

Intellectual property and WBL

As a WBL learner you might come up with creative ideas that could be exploited in some way, perhaps commercially. Who owns the rights to these ideas? Is it you, because you came up with the idea, or the university, which stimulated the creative thinking which led to the idea? This is what 'intellectual property' is about. All universities have policies to guide you on this, if the need arises, and your tutor will be able to put you in touch with the people concerned.

Plagiarism

Plagiarism is the representation of the ideas and words of others as your own. There are two main issues. Firstly, it's dishonest and mean. We should want to properly represent the ideas and words of others, giving full recognition to their ideas. Secondly, it is an act of ignorance. All of our ideas in professional work emerge from the work of others. If you think of research and ideas in our professions as conversations, we cannot make a meaningful contribution to the conversations if we do not know what conversations are taking place. Referencing in your written work is partly to show the reader that we know the current conversations and can add something to them, or inform our actions in relation to them. Not doing this suggests to the reader that we are ignorant of the conversations that are taking place in our field of practice.

To summarise, to behave ethically in university-level WBL contexts it is important that you think carefully about seeking informed consent from participants, ensuring sensitive commercial or business data remains confidential and generally 'doing no harm' in presenting material for assessment as well as all other aspects of your studies.

What does it mean to be an independent learner?

An independent learner – sometimes referred to as an autonomous or self-directed learner – can be seen as someone who assumes primary responsibility for their learning processes.

Being independent within a negotiated WBL programme will include taking the initiative throughout all the various phases of learning. Initially, this might include identifying learning opportunities from workplace activities and problems. Later, more detail will be needed in scoping out learning content and activities and how such learning could be evidenced and assessed. This is a demanding process of curriculum development and successfully organising yourself through such processes can lead you to major growth of self-confidence and pride in your achievements.

However, this is not to say that all work based learners in higher education begin their studies with high levels of independent self-direction and autonomy. Indeed, it is not always necessary to be highly self-directed in order to be a successful learner. Many learners, especially at the early stages of their WBL programmes, prefer to blend taught-on-campus or e-learning modules into their studies, in order to develop things like regular study habits that work for them, to compare themselves against a peer group and to understand more fully the expectations and language of higher education. The critical thing is to have a blend of learning you can feel comfortable with.

It's important to remember that independence does not mean isolation. Setting your own learning goals does not preclude you from having a close mentoring relationship from within your workplace to help you to identify useful opportunities from work, support resources, and so on. Such social concepts of learning from and with others in diverse social, organisational or professional contexts are often of paramount importance to learning. With university-level WBL, independent learning is a goal rather than an initial requirement.

You may also get to talk to other learners, either face to face or via online forums and discussion groups, or other uses of new technologies. Some universities have an online forum for work based learners, others have regular drop-in tutorial sessions. Some do both.

What does it mean to be a critical thinker?

Being a critical thinker involves more than logical reasoning or scrutinizing arguments for assertions unsupported by real evidence. Thinking critically involves recognizing the assumptions underlying our beliefs and behaviours. It means we can give justifications for our ideas and actions and importantly, it means we try to judge the rationality of these justifications.

WBL provides many opportunities and expectations for regular critical thinking. It offers the chance to engage in extended study of practice and, through dialogue and networking, to become involved in the development of communities of practice, which allow both theory and practice to be interrogated and related.

A very important element in ensuring that your WBL has a critical edge is the need to identify ideas and opinions from sources wider than your immediate situation and then to read, research, compare and contrast these sources with your own thinking. If you do not use such sources, then you are not underpinning your practice with theory, which is what HE is all about, even if this is not always expected in many workplaces.

What does it mean to be a reflective learner?

There is a substantial literature dealing with 'reflection' and we identify some of it in the section on Further Reading. If you want more detail than we provide here, then this will be your next port of call.

Reflective learning involves giving deliberate attention to cycles of enquiry, making space and time for thinking about complex and important issues. Conversationally, these cycles are often referred to as focusing on:

- WHAT?   an identification of the issue or problem;

- SO WHAT?   thinking about why the issue matters or what will be the benefit of solving or addressing it;

- NOW WHAT?   planning a way forward and acting on the plan.

Reflective learning also comes through discussions, reading, and practice. It can improve your knowledge and understanding and help you to look out for new opportunities to make a difference in your work performance.

Some useful tools for reflection are offered below. The list is not exhaustive, and tools can be combined in various ways.

Tools for Reflection

- **Critical incident analysis** – 'What? So What? Now What?' type questions are often involved, and it is important not to ignore the significance of feelings of those involved. Usually, a critical incident is an event where a new or deeper realisation occurs to you.

- **Keeping a journal** – This implies regular intervals and noting patterns and relationships with others over a period of time.

- **Keeping a learning log** – Learning logs are similar to journals, but tend to be seen as less systematic and more sporadic. You might make an entry to a learning log when you have completed an action and feel the impulse to write. However, both journals and learning logs review feelings, thoughts, ideas and actions, to make connections between them.

- **Selecting a specific focus of inquiry** – This will focus on some issue of professional importance to you and will involve working systematically through questions such as the 5Ws – Who? What? Where? When? Why? – plus How?

- **Mind mapping** – Mind mapping can help you to gain a wide overview of factors related to a problem – or an opportunity. Mind mapping often appeals to those who like visual pictures and schema. Factors can be grouped and linked to explore possibilities and to clarify perceptions and learning.

- **Action planning** – This will include consideration of what is desirable and feasible, and how you will know if your planned actions are having the desired effect.

How will I be assessed?

What many learners really appreciate about assessment practice in WBL is the input they can have into designing what evidence they will produce to meet the agreed learning outcomes. The formats of assignments can include reports, essays, dissertations and portfolios, but can also encompass more active presentations and exhibitions or shows. WBL learners also appreciate the opportunity to align assessments to real work projects, and to gain formative feedback from the workplace as well as from tutors. The diversity of assessments can also provide motivation as it enables people to design from their strengths rather than being assessed in inappropriate ways that do not relate to the work context.

Whatever the format of evidence you present, the main approach to all HE assessment is for the marking tutor to ask whether the work achieves the specified learning outcomes, and to check that your performance is at the expected level of academic study (see below) and meets any other more detailed assessment criteria which may be have been agreed or set down. You will have been advised approximately how many words (or equivalent) you need to produce and this will obviously vary depending on the number of credits involved (although it is worth pointing out that there is unlikely to be an exact requirement of so many words to achieve so many credits).

Try to avoid these common pitfalls in writing assignments:

- using a writing style, which is too conversational or informal. Most assignments require a more formal style of language, avoiding colloquialisms and slang terms;

- assuming that the reader knows your work context and practice and giving insufficient explanation;

- giving lengthy descriptions of an event, rather than analysing the significance of the event in terms of your underlying learning.

Your assignment will also be marked and graded according to the grading scheme within your university. Occasionally some negotiated modules are marked as pass or fail rather than graded. Work is then internally moderated or second marked to ensure the consistency or comparability of tutor assessments. Finally, assignments go forward for consideration by external examiners prior to the submission of results for each assessment board. Grades determine degree classifications for undergraduate qualifications or 'Pass', 'Merit' or 'Distinction' categories in Masters' degrees. You can be reassured that all your work will be expected to meet the same standards and go through the same processes as any other university qualifications. Results are quality assured through standard mechanisms that apply across all universities. When you have achieved major qualifications, you will be invited to a graduation ceremony to celebrate your success.

Usually, a limited number of draft pieces of work may be submitted to your tutor for formative assessment and feedback before final submission for assessment. You should agree with your tutor the process for doing this. Feedback on your final submission of work is provided to you after assessment and is designed to indicate to you how you can improve for future assignments. So it is a good idea to keep feedback for future reference in order to improve.

Assessment board schedules will provide you with target dates for completion and submission of work, so you will need to take note of these and make sure they get into your diary. You should plan your assessment so that you have time to spare to deal with any last minute hitches. If you encounter time problems and think that you may miss a planned assessment board you will need to find out the procedures and criteria in your university for asking for extensions or the penalties for late submission. If you do fail an assignment for any reason, you will usually be offered an opportunity to re-submit by a specific date so don't panic. Use the feedback given on why your work failed and what you need to do to improve it.

You may well be expected to use your access to the university web-based student portal to check your results and grades, and accept any opportunities for re-submissions, so make sure you know how to do this.

Levels of academic study

Through the Framework for Higher Education Qualifications (FHEQ), the Quality Assurance Agency for Higher Education (QAA) publishes reference points for standards of achievement at all higher education levels. Go to: http://www.qaa.ac.uk/ and then follow the links to: Standards and Quality/ Frameworks for Higher Education Qualifications.

These are generic statements applicable to all higher education programmes. Ufi/Learndirect has, as part of its higher education Learning through Work (LtW) programme http://www.learningthroughwork.org/ developed these general statements to create descriptions and indicators for work based learning. These do not apply to all university-level WBL programmes, but we include them because they systematically relate the general reference points for higher education to the specific area in which you are engaged.

Each level has an overall description, showing, at a general level, the kinds of things you will need to do to study at that level. There are also detailed 'indicators' for each level of study, covering five main areas.

Five main indicators for each level of study

- **Complexity and responsibility** – This concerns the level of complexity you are dealing with and what you are personally taking responsibility for (which can be different from the responsibility expected in your job);

- **Scope** – This is about whether you are for instance working within a closely defined situation or considering wider implications and impact;

- **Thinking and understanding** – This refers to the level of thinking and understanding you are using in analysing information, pulling information together and making decisions about what you are doing;

- **Investigation and evaluation** – This concerns how you are investigating information and evaluating situations;

- **Innovation and originality** – This is about the level of originality and innovation you are bringing to your work.

The following summaries show what is expected at each level. For more detailed level descriptors see Appendix, page 87.

Level 4 (Higher Education level 1; Certificates)

At Level 4, you will be thinking through and reviewing courses of action, making informed judgements on issues which affect your work and coping effectively with a range of unfamiliar situations and problems. You will need to be able to use your understanding of principles that apply to your work, as well as producing your own ideas and developing innovative responses. You will need to be able to carry out small-scale practical investigations, and review the appropriateness of different options.

Level 5 (Higher Education level 2; Foundation degrees and Diplomas)

At Level 5, you will be thinking through and reviewing courses of action, including their impact outside of your immediate work. You will be making informed judgements on issues which affect your work and coping effectively with a range of unfamiliar situations and problems. You will need to be able to draw on a broad personal or formal knowledge base and set of concepts which apply to your work, as well as producing your own ideas and developing innovative responses. You should be able to develop your own theories and find ways forward when faced with contradictions and dilemmas. You will need to be able to carry out small-scale practical research in relation to your work.

Level 6 (Higher Education level 3; Ordinary and Honours degrees)

At Level 6, you will be thinking through, understanding and reviewing different courses of action, including their impact outside of your immediate area of work. You will be making informed judgements on issues which affect your work, and working effectively with unpredictable issues. You will need to be able to draw on a broad personal or formal knowledge-base as well as concepts, theories and models which apply to your work. You will be producing your own ideas and practical theories, and developing innovative responses to complex situations. You should be able to manage dilemmas and find ways forward in problematic situations. You will need to be able to design and make use of practical, methodologically sound research to contribute to your work or that of your organisation.

Level 7 (Higher Education level 4; Postgraduate awards)

At Level 7, you will be developing thought-through courses of action which take into account alternative implications and issues beyond your immediate area of practice. You will be making informed judgements on issues which affect your work, and working effectively with unpredictable issues. You will need to be able to draw on mastery of a broad personal or formal knowledge base relating to the area of your work and its wider context, as well as developing and evaluating concepts, theories and models which apply to your work. You will be producing your own ideas and practical theories, and developing innovative responses in complex and unpredictable situations; you should be able to manage dilemmas and value-conflicts and find ways forward in problematic situations. One of the features of this level is that you will need to consider issues beyond your immediate area of practice, and take a critical approach to the thinking and assumptions which you and others are using. You will need to be able to design and make use of practical, methodologically sound research to contribute to your work or that of your organisation.

Level 8 (Higher Education level 5; Doctoral awards)

At Level 8, you will be developing thought-through courses of action which take into account alternative implications and issues beyond your professional discipline or area of practice. You will be making informed judgements on issues which affect your discipline or area of practice, and working effectively with unpredictable issues. You will need to be able to draw on critical and creative mastery of a broad range of concepts, theories and practices, as well as being aware of the assumptions underlying them from perspectives which go beyond individual disciplines and contexts. You will be producing your own ideas and theories and developing innovative responses in complex and unpredictable situations; you should be able to manage dilemmas and value-conflicts and find ways forward in problematic situations, including those which go beyond your organisation or discipline. One of the features of this level is that you will be taking forward an area of practice in a way which is of value beyond your organisation or community of practice, and developing as a leading practitioner in your field. You will need to be able to design and make use of practical, methodologically sound research which contributes to your area of practice, and which results in new understandings or approaches which extend or redefine existing knowledge or practice.

You can see from these kinds of level descriptors that university-level WBL is about developing and embedding critical thinking and reflection into your practice. This means that in the assessed work you undertake you will be expected to give very careful attention to words, the ideas they express and the assumptions that underpin actions too.

We'd like to finish this chapter on a positive note by encouraging you to feel confident in your WBL studies. Take the advice you're offered, ask if you're not sure, take one step at a time and you can do it!

Expectations and Support

Who is involved in my WBL programme?

During your time as a work based learner there will be a range of people who will be involved in providing support or who will be affected by your learning. One of the first questions to ask would be, 'Why am I doing this?' There could be a number of answers. You could be doing this in response to your own personal and professional needs or it may be a requirement from your employer in order to upskill and meet the challenges that your organisation faces. Keys to success in work based learning include taking ownership of your learning, being clear of its purpose and embracing the opportunity to spend time learning in the context of your work. In this way you will feel the benefit both personally and professionally. Being proactive is essential. You will have tutors so use them! All universities have a full support infrastructure in place (libraries, online resources, learner support etc). You should draw upon these resources. Your employer has the organisational and business knowledge and they may be able to provide support and guidance. You should make the most of opportunities to build contacts and relationships with experts and key stakeholders.

Important elements to your learning will be you, your employer, and the university but others involved include for your work colleagues, family and friends. There are significant implications for them too.

What is expected of me?

Work based learning in higher education is meant to be demanding on you, to stretch you and to challenge you. Although your programme will be based around the context of your workplace enabling you to undertake some learning activities in work time, there will also be a need to commit some of your own time in the evenings and at weekends.

You might expect to commit up to two evenings a week or a day at the weekend on your studies.

> **CASE STUDY**
>
> Frank is a teacher:
>
> *'I found that the amount of time I spent studying, and when I studied, varied a lot. It depended on schedules at work, my family, and the deadlines for assignments. It worked best for me when I planned ahead the times I would set aside for studying'.*

Are there any particular skills I need to have?

> **CASE STUDY**
>
> Kate is a drama teacher:
>
> *'I do not believe there are any special skills other than a belief in what you can achieve and a willingness to listen and learn.'*

However, to be a really successful work based learner, there are a number of key characteristics, which you need to acquire. You need to be:

- motivated;
- an independent learner;
- enquiring;
- proactive;
- dedicated;
- forward thinking;
- organised;
- a good time keeper;

- informed;

- a good communicator;

- able to work with others.

It may be useful to look at this list to identify where your strengths lie. You may also identify additional characteristics that apply. Don't worry if you don't feel that you have all of these at the moment as these can be included as a feature of your individual programme of study.

CASE STUDY

Lauren leads a multidisciplinary team in social care. She found that many of the skills that she used in her job, particularly being proactive and organised, helped her with her studying. She had a plan of what she was going to do and roughly by when she would do it, in order to help her to maintain her momentum. By taking this proactive approach to planning her learning, blocking time in her diary and regularly contacting her tutor with a progress update, she was able to progress even though she was busy, as she had allocated time to do her work. The plan also enabled her to schedule work tasks and family activities, and then review and refine her work.

'Taking time to plan my project to fit around my work and family has given me confidence to say NO on occasions when I really needed to focus on my study.'

You will be expected to read, make notes and undertake assignments related to your work. Relating what you have read to what is happening or could happen in your work will be a key element of your programme. You will be expected to read from a variety of sources such as academic books, journal articles and conference papers, professional and governmental publications as well as reputable internet sources. **Reading is a critical factor for success in higher education**. Reading will broaden your ideas and perspective and should enable you to think of the wider implications associated with your work and organisation.

How well motivated am I?

To be successful, you need to be or become a highly motivated active learner. Motivation manifests itself in many different ways. You must be able to work autonomously, to take responsibility for identifying your learning needs and aspirations and for managing and driving the learning process. Normally, in order to do this you will need to draw upon, use and develop significant prior work experience and professional knowledge. You will need to develop and utilise appropriate learning and enquiry methods along with project management skills, and to investigate and integrate the relationship between academic theory and workplace practice. All of the above is bound within the process of critical reflection. As a learner, the more motivated you are the more productive and creative your work will be. At all times you will be in charge of your learning experience and it will be your responsibility to approach your tutor and be aware of your assignment submission dates etc.

How will I fit this into my life?

Making the time and space in your life for this work is very important. A belief in what you want to achieve and that you can do it is important because of the amount of work that will be involved.

> **CASE STUDY**
>
> Brendan sums this up:
>
> *'I have found that I have to really want to do this. It doesn't really take over your life but it becomes a very big part of it as you need to spend a lot of time thinking about and planning what there is to do as well as the time actually doing it.'*

Juggling work, home and study commitments can be a daunting prospect, but it is possible – thousands of people in this situation have successfully gained qualifications whilst working and learning. It just takes some careful planning. There are a few simple things that you can do to help you to achieve this.

Why not use things that you are doing at work as a basis for your learning and assessment? Look for opportunities to use work projects which excite you and that are manageable and realistic. WBL projects need to be beneficial to you and your organisation and should enable you to both work and learn. When you choose university modules that are to be part of and support your programme of study, make sure you choose those that are going to be interesting and useful. By doing some extra reading and spending time thinking about this reading in relation to your job you can then present this as a part of your assessed work.

CASE STUDY

As John, an engineer comments:

'From the company's point of view, part of the reason why they're sponsoring me is because they see that it actually fits with the work I do here and whatever I do will actually be of benefit, not only to me, but also to the company.'

Consider what is happening within your organisation and align your work based studies with your organisational objectives. Discuss your proposals with your line manager in order that you are both developing your knowledge and producing tangible benefits to the organisation.

CASE STUDY

Stephen, undertaking an undergraduate management programme believes that:

'Input and support from the employer is vital when doing WBL as it is necessary to get direction to what is in the learning plans and by making it fit into the actual work undertaken it means that the time spent on actual work becomes time spent on the learning and the modules. There is also the possibility that the learning undertaken can relate more to the future your employer sees for you and similarly that you see and want for yourself. It is relevant to have a sponsor who can understand what you are doing and what it means to undertake the work.'

Talk to your tutor about the possibilities of how your prior learning gained from your experience could be incorporated into your work or be used to exempt you from part of the programme. They will help you to ascertain whether you can do this and guide you through the process.

Gustav, who works in logistics, said that his work based project not only helped him towards the qualification, it also improved what he did for work because he had spent more time thinking about other possible solutions:

'I think if I'd have done it just as a work project, I wouldn't have done the reading and have gained the level of knowledge that I've done as part of this programme.'

Find a support network of people to help you. Talk to your work colleagues and friends, and other learners to get hints and tips from others who have combined working and learning.

Colleagues may offer to proof read your work for you or to talk through ideas for a project or assessed piece of work – take them up on it! Your work colleagues may be able to help you formulate your ideas and frame your thinking in relation to your reading. This need not be as a formal tutorial or a long discussion – often a chat over a coffee can be very helpful and begin a chain of thought. Sharing your ideas can also give you an insight into other people's perceptions as they may see possibilities and difficulties that you have not foreseen. Colleagues may also have come upon useful articles or reading that may help you.

Just as important, however, is the offer from friends to socialise occasionally. Sometimes you can become so immersed in work that you become too close to it. Giving yourself some space can allow your thoughts to develop, and allow you to see your work in a new light.

Plan, prioritise and compromise! You must prepare for your studies and planning is a key factor in all WBL programmes and modules. Planning will help you to identify issues that may compete for your time. Make sure that you have identified the key dates related to your studies and build them into your schedule. Identify your priorities and look at those that can be moved and those that can't.

According to Oliver, a design manager, planning is a crucial part of your study:

'...making the time and space in your life for this work is very important. Planning what will be done and understanding what it is to achieve helps to relate to it and the effort it needs. A belief in what you want to achieve and that you can do it is important because of the amount of work that will be involved.'

Remember to balance other activities with your learning. For example, it may be possible to delay a regular work task for a short period in order to meet a study deadline or you may need to get academic work finished in advance of your study deadline in order to make time to do something for work.

Oussama works in Finance and as a work based learner, was studying an online module as a part of his work based programme. The deadline for submission for all learners was at the end of March. Working in the finance department of a public company, the end of March is an extremely busy time, as this coincides with the preparation of the end of year accounts. Oussama planned his study so that he could complete his assignment earlier than the deadline.

What is expected of my family and friends?

Support from your family and friends is important, because their lives will be affected by your study and they too may have to compromise on the time that they spend with you. They can help you to create the time and environment that you need to study. However, sometimes as well as giving you space to work it is important that they give you the opportunity for a break, as well as supplying you with endless cups of tea and biscuits!

It is important that you create a suitable environment to work at home. You need time and a suitable work space. Try and assign regular study periods every week. In this way your family can see that this is your study time and know not to disturb you. You need to keep your papers together in a safe place. Lever arch files are very useful in these circumstances. Secure online filing is also important. In return for this organisation your family will know that these things are important and not to interfere with, delete or 'tidy' them away. It is very frustrating to find that the crucial article for your studies has been used as material for your child's latest origami project!

Family can also help on a practical level, proof reading drafts to check for spelling and grammatical errors as well as checking that what you have written has a logical flow.

> **CASE STUDY**
>
> As Sally comments:
>
> *'I discovered that my teenage son was an absolute whiz at creating tables and diagrams on the computer, and showed me how to do it with much patience, proud (and just a little smug) that for once he could advise me about my homework!'*

> **CASE STUDY**
>
> Aminder is a project manager and is doing a degree in Applied Business Studies by negotiated WBL. She has learned that sitting at the computer with her study papers has had a positive effect on her children:
>
> *'Sitting down to do my work in a quiet space and organising my materials has set my children a good example. I find that they have started to do the same with their school work.'*

It is important however that you strike a balance between work, home life and study. Inevitably unforeseen events do occur when family members have problems or may be ill for a long period of time. In such circumstances it is very important that you contact your tutor to inform them of the situation, as they may be able to offer moral support or the potential for extension. They will certainly be able to offer guidance about the university regulations on such matters.

What can I expect of my employer?

Many individuals who take up higher education work based learning do so at the behest of their employer. Here, the employer will have more than likely engaged with the university to develop a work based programme that meets one or more organisational needs, for example, the development of some specific skills in response to an organisational or policy driven initiative. Usually the programme will be developed for and offered to a range of people in the organisation. The university and employer will have taken some considerable time in planning and developing the programme before the learners enrol and will have agreed the responsibilities of each organisation. An effective partnership working culture is an essential ingredient for success where each partner brings a range of expert knowledge, experience, skill, capacity and resources. They should have agreed their responsibilities with respect to the delivery, assessment, learner support and evaluation of the programme.

One university has developed a work based programme with a large NHS foundation trust. The trust wanted to use a work based approach with staff from across the organisation to address key NHS priorities around improving the patient journey, multi-professional working and improving working lives. The university and the trust agreed their respective responsibilities, where the trust provided:

- publicity and recruitment information;
- expert advice;
- line management support;
- work based advisors;
- use of IT training;
- study time;
- library support.

However some people take up WBL as an individual learner. In such situations, not all learners are keen for their employers to know that they are doing this or wish for them to be involved in their learning. This may be, for example, because the learning is designed to enable a career move. In such situations, learners can find that they are more limited in what they can do within their programme of study. If you are in this situation it would be wise to speak to a university WBL tutor in advance. He/she will be able to give you the appropriate advice as to whether your intended study is feasible.

Work based learning, whilst designed to enable you to study what interests you and what is relevant to you and your job, can also be hugely beneficial to your organisation. It will not only gain an enhanced practitioner but also your work is likely to have a direct impact on the effectiveness of your organisation.

Talk to your manager about study time. People often make assumptions that their manager won't give them time off for study. A good place to start is by understanding your organisation's policy on study time entitlements and how you arrange this. Ask your Human Resources department if you have one. The manager is more likely to agree study time where he/she can see tangible benefits. If this is arranged around organisational priorities, it is more likely for such requests to be dealt with sympathetically.

CASE STUDY

Penny, a nurse on a busy ward, recognised that she couldn't have regular time off for study, but asked her manager if she could have a study day about a month before her assignment submission date. She gave her manager plenty of notice before the shift rota had been prepared, making some suggestions for suitable days, having first checked the ward holiday chart and admissions list. When her manager realised that Penny was prepared to be flexible about the actual date, she agreed that she could have a day for study. During the course of the conversation it became apparent to her manager that the patient information leaflet that Penny was preparing for the assessment could be of good use on the ward. She also made some suggestions to Penny on background reading and offered to proof read the work for her.

As a work based learner it is helpful to have additional support within your workplace. Your employer may act as, or suggest a work based mentor to help you in your programme of study. In some university programmes it is a requirement that you must have a work based mentor.

A work based mentor might:

- help you to cope with ongoing change and the increasing complexities and challenges of the workplace;

- broaden your perspective and your abilities to commit to working life;

- give you access to a person with greater experience, who can provide comprehensive assistance;

- help you to improve your self-confidence and self-esteem in achieving objectives.

Help from your employer

Your employer might:

- give you basic encouragement and support to help you learn and progress;

- provide equipment and materials, such as a computer with internet access and access to information and documents;

- enable some flexibility in your working patterns and allow for study time;

- give assistance with fees;

- provide a work based mentor or specialist expertise as required

- give help and advice on work based projects;

- advise on aspects of business confidentiality or ethics which may arise from your studies;

- help with personal and professional development planning;

- provide in-house continuing professional development which is relevant to your study;

- direct you to relevant information and expertise.

What if I am self-employed?

If you are self-employed or work in short-term employment (for example, such as those in the entertainment industry or project workers), you won't have an employer. However, this does not preclude you from WBL – you will simply look elsewhere for the necessary support. For example, a work based mentor does not need to be someone with whom you work, but could be a colleague from a different organisation or department who works in a similar field to you. Whilst tuition fees might be more of a burden (see Chapter 5) you won't have to negotiate a work/study balance with an employer.

What support can I expect from the university?

You can expect the university to provide you with a starting point and explanation of the process you will go through. This is particularly important for you as a work based learner, as you may often be working on your own. Receiving clear information from your tutor about the programme is also essential for those who are perhaps returning to academic learning after a very long time or who may not have undertaken formal study since leaving school. You should make use of the vast array of university resources, including an extensive electronic library, lots of web based support material and advice from friendly and helpful staff including your own tutor. The university will provide information on what support can be accessed and how your relationship with your tutor will work in practice. It will provide you with a handbook, which will provide details about the university resources, the programme of study, study requirements, regulations and timetables etc. It can be beneficial to have a half or whole day at the university as a start to the process to cover these points and perhaps to discuss the development of your programme. On some programmes there will be a formal induction programme that you may be required to attend with other work based learners.

Universities have a wide range of resources available but, as with all service based organisations, you need to learn how to access and use them effectively.

CHAPTER FIVE:
Understanding Universities

This section aims to introduce you to some important aspects of studying at university as a work based learner. It is important to understand that universities normally run programmes of study where attending classes on campus has been considered the usual approach. This means university systems are based on the expectation that students will attend a university campus on a weekly basis. University systems and practices based on this expectation will make perfectly reasonable demands of campus based students, for example, to visit the library to pick up your student identity card. For this reason, the administrative systems, and sometimes the academic structures often do not cater well for part-time, work based learners. Many universities are making good progress towards the improvements needed, but it is important, as a WBL learner, that you understand this, make adjustments in your expectations and develop tactics to make sure you get what you need to make your studies a success. This is the focus of this section: understanding universities and the practical things you need to do to be a successful WBL learner.

What does all the jargon mean?
Universities use particular terms and abbreviations to make it easier for people working in universities to do their work. Generally, people in universities including academics and administrators use particular terms and abbreviations to help them to be clear with each other. The intention is not to make you feel excluded. However, all the jargon, unfamiliar terms and abbreviations can easily have that effect. It is important to spend the time needed to understand the terms and abbreviations. This will mean reading carefully the information sent to you by the university to help you with your studies. If you do not understand a particular word,

term or abbreviation, you need to refer to glossaries, Frequently Asked Questions (FAQs) and other information provided by the university to understand what is meant by the specific term. If you are unsure, ask, as sometimes a quick phone call can clear up any confusion. To help you with some of the most common terms and their abbreviations, we have included a Glossary of Terms that attempts to define and explain 'terms' used across the higher education sector (see Glossary of Terms page 75).

How do I choose the right university and programme for me?

What are you looking for from your work based learning (WBL) studies programme? Is it relevance to your workplace, distance learning possibilities, being able to share in the design of your own study plan, or a combination of such things? With a clear idea of what you want, you are better prepared to explore possibilities.

Different universities approach WBL in different ways, but they all tend to stress the fact that you play an active part in designing your programme, and that there must be relevance to your work role. When we say 'work' however, this does not necessarily mean paid employment. You might be working in a voluntary capacity that offers similar challenges and opportunities to a paid working role.

The idea of a 'learning agreement' is common. This means that you work with your employer and the university to create an agreement concerning what you will study, how you will do it and over how long a period of time.

You need to be prepared for the fact that some universities do not offer a WBL option at all in the sense that we have defined it in this book. Not all universities recognise the workplace as a source of learning, and they may simply have nothing to offer. Others may have good WBL provision but it may not be obvious. It may be hidden, for example, under a 'lifelong learning' heading.

You may feel that you need to include some specialist modules taught on campus as part of your study, so that you have the reassurance of attending the university for at least part of your course – this should always be a possibility in a good work based learning programme so it is something to look out for.

Also consider the responsiveness of the university to you as a customer. Can you find information about WBL easily on the website? When you call them for advice, is it easy to get? Are they able to put you in touch with a person who can explain how the WBL programme will work in your case, and can they send you some material to explain it all? Can they recognise previous courses that you already have credit for and help you build that work into your programme? Do they sound as if they know what they have to offer and what is in it for you and your employer? Crucially, can they tell you how much it will cost!

Finding a university that offers WBL

A small number of universities offer a WBL route to most or all of their subjects. A greater number offer specific WBL routes within specific subjects. Because WBL programmes do not appear on UCAS (the admissions service for universities) you will need to visit university websites to check what is available. Our advice is to start with your local university and to use web-based searches to find the universities that offer WBL that match your needs. By trying different combinations of searches you will find the universities that offer WBL either in your local area, or in subjects you wish to focus on.

What's in it for my employer?

WBL is an attractive option for many employers. It usually needs very little time spent away from the workplace on study days, and it gives the learner a chance to do something that can make a real difference at work.

It may be, therefore, that your employer is already aware of a WBL study option, and is prepared to fund it, knowing that they have a stake in the outcomes. Some WBL programmes make the relationship between learner and employer formal, requiring that the employer not only understands what the learner is doing, but also is committed to supporting it. This might mean that a bit of thoughtful lobbying on your part might help your employer look favourably on funding you. Think about how your studies might contribute to your appraisal targets or to your departmental or organisational objectives – these things make the point that WBL can really make a difference at work.

Can I learn at a distance?

For many learners, the point of taking a WBL programme is that there is often no requirement to attend the university or college concerned. Many courses can be partially or completely undertaken at a distance, but you need to check if there are any special attendance needs. You also need to be aware that there are sometimes different interpretations of what is meant by WBL. Some institutions use the term but mean that attendance at the university is consolidated in the workplace, and you need to clarify just how the university concerned is defining the term. Your chosen university should have a Virtual Learning Environment (VLE) through which you are able to study entirely at a distance. If the VLE includes a learner discussion board, you can become one of a group of mutually supportive people learning together and sharing their experience and insight even though they never meet face to face. This is important as a work based learner, as you may have a lot to offer others, but you can also gain from their knowledge and insight. Remember that the point of WBL is that your learning is drawn from your own reflection on your experience. In effect, you already know much of what needs to be known about your work practice and you do not need someone to teach you the theory needed to help you to do your job. You just need help to explore and explain your learning, and to put it in an academic framework.

Can I mix distance learning with study on the university campus?

For some learners, a WBL module may form just one part of a course, which does ask you to attend certain modules. This often happens with courses that have a clear subject specialism, such as Criminology or Tourism, where the WBL module complements the specialist modules taught on campus. The mixture of on-campus 'taught' modules plus distance learning, supported by technological resources is called 'blended learning', which is increasingly common in higher education. This mixture can offer you the benefit of specialist theoretical input from the university lecturers, added to the work related focus of the WBL activity – a powerful combination.

Will my previous study be recognised?

You may already have some university credits from previous study. Your chosen university should be able to recognise these through the process called accreditation of prior learning (APL, see glossary) and help you fit them within your study programme, as long as they are relevant. Make sure that you keep any certificates or other evidence that these credits have been awarded, as you may be asked to show this at some stage. It should not matter that you have been awarded these credits at a different university, as the credit accumulation and transfer system in the UK means that credits are transferable between many universities. Be aware that you will always need to complete a certain proportion of your studies, probably at least a third, at your chosen university.

Does the university have a lot of experience with WBL?

WBL is often misunderstood, being confused with work placements, which often have a very different focus as a carefully supervised introduction to a specialist workplace. It may sometimes appear, therefore, that the university offers more WBL than is the case when you start to explore in detail. As a work based learner, you should be asking yourself if the university could meet your needs. Is it flexible in what is on offer? Does it see you and your experience as the starting point for the development of the course concerned, or does it insist that you attend specific modules within a rigid study pattern? Does it really put your WBL first, or is there a feeling that what comes from the university is the only important learning? It takes a special kind of university to recognise that WBL can be equally as valuable academically as classroom learning. Universities that offer WBL in the ways in which we have defined it in this book are often at the cutting edge of educational innovation. They offer a relationship between you, your employer and the university that is not possible in more conservative institutions. You should be prepared to spend some time checking out university websites to see what is on offer.

Remember, if you or your employer are paying for your studies, you are a customer! Exercise your right to shop around. WBL staff often have a real passion for their work and are only too pleased to discuss individual learner needs and help you recognise how you could benefit from their course.

What are the different sorts of routes I could follow?

It is possible to study as a work based learner from Certificate level (1st year of university study) to doctorate level, although the doctoral qualification may have a different name such as DProf (Doctor of Professional Studies). All levels of qualification between these two are possible, and you may find that you can include WBL elements in other courses at various academic levels.

George is an administrator in a college. He is undertaking a Graduate Certificate in Student Support. The Certificate is run in partnership between the university and a group of local colleges. As part of the certificate, George will undertake a work based project to complement the other, campus taught modules. When George completes the certificate, he has the option to use the certificate towards a full degree.

It is also often possible to do 'stand alone' modules for continuing professional development purposes – this is especially useful when you need to complete a project at work but you may not necessarily want to move on to longer term study. Remember, though that you may well be able to use the credits gained if you decide to move on to further study later.

Will I have to buy lots of books and other materials?

Generally, no. Remember that WBL is not so much interested in your specific subject knowledge as in your ability to make clear your learning from work, so it is often not necessary to buy specific textbooks. Also remember that a single group of work based learners will include people from a wide range of work areas, each of which has its own academic literature, so specific books are hard to recommend. This does not mean, however, that you do not need to be familiar with any theory. In WBL, instead of the traditional academic sequence of learning the theory and then applying it at work, you are more likely to be asked to make clear your learning from work, then to find the theory which supports it and helps you to develop it. Also remember that many WBL projects have a focus on your workplace policy and practice, so some important documents may come from within your own organisation.

The university will give you access to its library and other learning resources, both campus based and online, and many academic journals, articles and other resources, such as government documents, are now available online. Universities offer a range of support services to learners working at a distance, often including financial advice and good support to help you develop your skills in using the electronic library and other services. If you belong to a union or a professional body, such as the Royal College of Nursing, they may have a library with online access. Your employers may also have their own academic support system including books and other resources.

If there is an exception concerning specialist books, it may be related to research methods. If you are undertaking a WBL research methods module at a high academic level, some good research methods texts will be recommended for the course, and some of these may well be worth buying for your exclusive use. Remember that one aim of WBL is to help you realise that your learning and development do not end when the course ends – you should be prepared to continue to learn and develop at work, which may involve working on further research and development projects, so the theory you become familiar with here should have lasting value.

What do I do if things go wrong?

The down side of flexibility can be complexity. WBL programmes can sometimes contain elements from more than one academic department within the university. This can mean that your course pathway can be 'non-standard'. It is important that you liaise closely with your tutor so that you understand exactly the planned sequence of events. You should be given the name of your tutor, who will be a member of academic staff in WBL, at the start of your studies. They may not teach or guide you on all of the modules that you undertake, but they are a continuing source of advice and support as you progress.

Universities are administratively complex organisations and there are a number of places where problems can occur. If you have problems linked to administration, your tutor can help you make contact with the right people at the right time, to avoid problems with things like paying fees, getting library and VLE access, and getting copies of essential learning materials. Things are often easier in a university that has a lot of WBL provision – the administrators and academic advisers concerned often know the systems well and can quickly sort out a problem. If problems continue, all universities have a complaints procedure that can be followed to make your dissatisfaction clear. Don't forget, though, that if you are in touch with other learners, they can often be a good source of information on how to work around the problems which crop up.

What are the consequences if I have problems coping with the course?

As a WBL learner, there is often more at stake for you than for learners on other courses. Your work colleagues will be aware that you are studying, and the expected outcomes of your work will have direct relevance to your workplace. Some of your colleagues will be more directly involved as they may be part of a project which you are including as part of your WBL studies. If you fail, therefore, everyone will know, so it is vital that you think through the implications of undertaking the course.

Ask yourself the following questions:

- Does my manager support me in my ambition to study and develop?

- Will my workplace give me time and space for the academic side of my studies?

- Will my workplace support me when I need to involve them in my studies?

- Do I feel that the university understands what is at stake for me?

- Do I feel that the university is aware of the realities of trying to study in my own workplace?

If you can answer yes to these questions, you are in a strong starting position. A university that understands WBL will know that things go wrong, both personally and professionally. They are used to the fact that people change jobs, fall ill, or get overwhelmed with work and all the multitude of other factors that affect the ability to study to a timetable. Your university tutor will be sympathetic and supportive if you keep them informed of developments, and can help you to refocus your studies as circumstances change. It is also vital, of course, that you keep your workplace up to date concerning your progress and your plans, especially if they are funding your studies.

What does it cost?

Paying for your WBL higher education is a serious issue, and is not something you will be considering lightly. This section aims to set out the money issues and provide explanations and some guidance as you consider a WBL programme.

Who pays?

Unlike standard, full-time higher education, the funding of a WBL programme may be more complex. It might mean as a learner you contribute nothing personally to the fees, or it might mean you fully fund your fees. You may get a career development loan, or your employer may make a contribution in money, or in kind. Who pays may be structured into the partnership between an employer and university, or subject to negotiation between a learner and their employer. As a WBL learner it is probably fair to say that all parties will look to shift the costs from their budget or income to someone else. Knowing this, you may well have to be flexible and negotiate carefully to ensure you limit the personal cost to you.

Does the government contribute money towards my WBL programme?

The government supports universities by making an annual payment to each university. This payment partly pays for teaching and the administration of each university and is based on each university teaching an agreed number of students per year. Therefore, as a WBL learner, part of the costs of your tuition and other costs like the university library services are paid directly by government. Whatever amount you personally pay or is paid by your employer or sponsor, the government will pay a significant part of the costs directly to the university. When the university publishes its fees, the fee is in addition to the amount already paid by direct government subsidy to the university.

Working for a large employer?

If the WBL programme is arranged in partnership with an employer, it is normal for the employer to pay some or all of the costs. This is especially true where the employer will realise the benefit of your education directly to the business. Where the employer sees the WBL programme as important training for you, you are more likely to get the fees paid in full. This is also true of employers in the public sector where education and development is part of their staff development strategy. However lots of different factors can influence your employer's decision, not least the general economic situation and the budgets available for training and development within the company or organisation.

If the employer does not fully pay fees for you, or pays only a contribution towards the fees, it is quite normal for the employer to either provide support for your learning, or allow some time off for studying. Where support is provided, the employer may feel this substitutes for paying fees. For example, the employer might make a workplace mentor available. Alternatively, the employer might allow time off for study where they are not able to fund your studies.

Therefore, the support from your employer depends on two points. Firstly, whether they are in partnership with the university and see your programme as a structured part of staff development in their organisation. Secondly, it may depend on their ability to pay or the extent to which they are familiar with the idea of developing their workforce through higher education programmes.

CASE STUDY

Of her employer, Sheila said:

'I started out paying for my degree but after the first project my employer took over the payments as he saw a clear business benefit.'

Working for a small company or organisation?

Many employees working for small to medium size companies (SMEs) engage in WBL. Many of them successfully fund their studies from a variety of sources. They are however, likely to take greater control over the decision to undertake WBL and responsibility for funding their studies compared with learners who are part of an employer partnership. If you are in this category, you may be less likely to find your employer willing to fund your studies, or to involve themselves in a partnership model of delivery with a university. However, you may find other ways to get your employer to support you. For example, by allowing flexible working so you can work and study at the same time. You may well find that the structure of your organisation allows you to negotiate directly with senior managers to get the maximum support of the type you feel is realistic for your employer to provide. The emphasis here is on negotiating the support you need by arguing for the benefits that the employer might realise when you complete your programme.

Self-employed?

As a self-employed person, you are much more likely to be viewing your WBL programme as a stepping stone to improve practice or career progression. You are balancing the effort and costs of study against the likely benefits that you will see at the end of your studies. Many self-employed people engage in WBL for very practical reasons, not least that for many, a WBL route is the only way to continue to work and to study at the same time. The focus here is on a judgement you make about the benefits set against the costs and risks. If you are in this category a simple evaluation of the likely positive and negative consequences of undertaking a WBL programme will help you make the decision whether to proceed or not. You will need to additionally consider your cash flow as fees become due. A career development loan may soften the impact on cash flow (see the section below on loans).

How do I get the correct fees information?

It is very important to understand the basis upon which fees are charged. You can get this information from the university but ensure that you get this in writing rather than from a telephone call. Universities publish

'Fee Schedules' or 'Fee Rates' that detail how they charge fees. Make sure you have a detailed and official document from the university that explains how fees will be charged and when. It is usually best to get this directly from the WBL unit in the university rather from the admissions department of the university as the WBL unit will usually have the correct information.

How are fees calculated?

Generally there are two approaches. The first is where the university charges a fee per module or unit. This charge usually falls due at the beginning of the term or semester in which you will take the module or unit. This method enables you to plan when to pay and how much to pay. The second approach is less common and involves an annual fee. You get charged the annual fee whatever your progress on the programme. You pay every year until you graduate. This second method is more common in older universities and at postgraduate level. Do note that with both approaches, published fees will go up each year, so the fee for a module you will be taking next year will be slightly higher when you come to pay because the published fees are updated on an annual basis.

Where do I go for information on financial support?

If you are liable to pay fees for your WBL programme, there is a range of possible funding sources that can partly, and in some instances, substantially offset the cost to you. The Directgov website is the official government website for citizens and provides up to date and detailed information about financial support: http://www.direct.gov.uk/. You should check out the current information by following the links on the Directgov website to: Education and Learning / University and higher education / Student finance.

Am I eligible for a grant?

Firstly you may be eligible for a non-repayable grant for part-time study that covers part of your fees, provided you normally live in England or Wales. This is definitely worth applying for if you are just starting out in your professional work, or if you work in a sector where salaries are low or contract work is intermittent. For example, if you are just starting out in the performing arts sector, you may find you are on a low income. You may well be eligible for a grant as the grant is means tested. That is, a grant may be payable if your income is low. Clearly this is much better than the option for full-time students who can only get a loan that is repayable. Grants are non-repayable and therefore should be highly prized! Details are available from the Directgov website.

Am I eligible for a loan?

Another source of funding is from the Career Development Loan Scheme. This offers repayable loans similar to the Student Loan Scheme but is designed for people in work who will be studying part time. You may well consider this option if you are earning a reasonable income which would exclude you from a grant. Generally if you are in part-time work that pays a reasonable salary, or in full-time work, you are unlikely to get a grant, but are likely to be eligible for a Career Development Loan. Details are available from the Directgov website.

Am I eligible for a bursary or scholarship?

Increasingly, universities offer bursaries to support learners, especially where they have been able to get an external body or individual to pay for the scholarship or bursary. Generally, a bursary is a payment made towards your overall costs, for example, towards travel, or books. A scholarship is most often a payment of your fees in full. Each university is responsible for its bursaries and scholarships, so you should follow the links on the university website, and follow up with a telephone call to the scholarship and bursaries office in your chosen university or universities.

What additional guidance is available to me about financial support?

All universities provide a money and welfare advice service with information and advisers who can help you. However, the quality of guidance may vary from university to university. Go directly to the university website for links to their money and welfare advice service.

So how do I handle getting the right information?

You may do best to go to the WBL central unit if such a thing exists as they may have the up-to-date and correct information. You might need to pursue the issue of fees, financial support and guidance in a fairly persistent manner to get the information you need. You may experience better support and guidance at a university that has a large WBL provision, although there are no guarantees. Be persistent, and compare the information from different sources to see what seems to be the agreed information, and be prepared to experience some frustrations as you navigate the complexity. Find the individual at the university who seems willing to help you and pump them relentlessly for information! Have clear questions, as they are more likely to get clear responses. Try and find the more senior person to ask. They will either know the answer to your question, or know someone who does, and are less likely to avoid you, as they are likely to have greater responsibility to ensure the smooth running of WBL programmes. Be polite, but persistent as universities are very complex organisations and you may have a non-standard question that only certain individuals will be able to answer.

Glossary of Terms

Accreditation of Prior Experiential Learning (APEL)
This is the process by which an individual learner can obtain academic credits for learning developed from experiences at work or in professional practice. The university assesses the learning by comparing it with similar learning that might have taken place on campus.

Accreditation of Prior Learning (APL)
This is the process by which an individual learner can obtain academic credits for learning achieved on formal courses and training (e.g. a HND counting towards a BA degree).

Admissions
The university department that takes enquiries from potential students, receives applications and processes these.

Blended Learning
A mode of study made popular by the Open University where learners mostly study at a distance, but with some campus sessions and some online learning. The balance between these can vary, and sometimes can be negotiated with your tutor.

Board of Studies
Official body in each university where teachers and learners discuss the concerns of learners and make a record of these for action to be taken. It is an important forum for the learner voice to be heard. All academics must demonstrate they listen to, and take action to address concerns raised at Board of Studies.

Credits and Credit Points
University qualifications are made up of specific amounts of credits. You need to complete the specified number of credits to achieve a particular qualification. So for example, to gain a Bachelors degree with honours (BA Hons) you need to successfully complete 360 credits. Credits in higher education can be transferred between universities.

Distance Learning	A mode of study where you do not attend the university for 'lectures' but where the 'learning' and the 'teaching' are run in separate locations. Your tutor may be in her office at the university while you undertake your studies at home or in the workplace. Distance learners usually have learning materials specifically designed for this mode of study.
Enrolment	The process by which you agree to take the place on the programme and accept the responsibility to pay any fees.
Formative Assessment	This is where a tutor assesses a learner's performance or work to provide feedback on how improvements can be made. It is usually undertaken at points during the course of a module or unit.
Higher Education	This is the highest level of education available provided by special institutions that are either universities, university colleges or other specialist centres that deliver higher education. The term is interchangeable with 'university-level'.
Higher Education Institution (HEI)	A university, university college or other institution that has been granted the right to make UK Higher Education Awards by the Privy Council.
Induction	The process by which the university introduces you to its systems, regulations and support available to you as a learner. This is often campus based, but may be virtual or through documents sent to you by post.
Learning Materials	Handbooks and study materials given to you so you can follow a particular module or unit. This might include a Reader (see Reader) and a list of suggested reading.
Learning Resources	The term used to describe university services that support learning. These will include library services, email and access to the university network. Can also include placement services, careers advice etc.
Mode of Study	Universities deliver their programmes in significantly different 'modes' which include 'full time'; 'part time'; 'on campus', 'flexible learning'; 'distance learning'. This may have greater importance to the university and their funding arrangements than your experience as a learner. It may have fee and funding implications for you.
Modules or Units	The parts that make up a university qualification. They are usually followed in a specific sequence towards a specific qualification title. There may be 'core' modules / units which you must successfully complete, and 'optional' modules / units which you can choose from as part of your programme.

National Qualifications Framework	The list of academic and vocational qualifications and an attempt to indicate the equivalence between vocational and academic qualifications.
NVQ	National Vocational Qualifications (NVQs) are work-related, competency-based qualifications. They do not reflect the higher level learning skills of higher education, but place emphasis on specific skills and knowledge for particular jobs.
Negotiated Modules or Units	Modules or Units where the focus of the studies is negotiated between you, the university, and often your employer (if applicable).
Online Learning	A university programme run entirely using a web-based system.
Programme / Programme of Study	The series of modules you undertake in order to reach your target qualification. The programme may include, or be made up entirely of negotiated modules / units.
Programme Leader	Member of academic staff with responsibility for leading the delivery of a whole WBL or traditional programme at undergraduate or postgraduate level.
Qualifications	These are 'certificated' awards made by universities, colleges and professional training organisations. University qualifications have a range of titles that are usually linked to the academic level.
Reader	A handbook with extracts from books and other literature which you are expected to read and use as part of a module or unit.
Registration	The process by which you apply to become a learner at university. This means making an application for a programme of study, course or module. After sending in an application form, you are likely to be asked to sign a letter confirming you would like to accept the place on the programme.
Registry	The university department which holds the information on learners, the programmes they are following, their grades, and their final award.
Semesters / Terms	Most universities organise teaching into two semesters or three terms per year. Each is followed by a period in which official assessment of learners' work is undertaken. Semesters run late September to end of December and late January to mid May. Terms normally run in the Autumn, Winter and Spring, as in schools.

Summative Assessment	This is where a tutor (and sometimes the workplace) assesses a learner's performance or work to grade it. It is usually undertaken at the end of a module or unit and 'sums up' achievement. You will normally receive feedback to help you understand how the grading has been made.
Tutor	The tutor is the academic who runs the modules you are taking as part of your course. They may also be known as: Programme Adviser, Academic Advisor, Academic Supervisor etc.
Tutorial	One to one or small group meeting with a university tutor. It may be in person, by telephone, video-link or online.
University-level	A term that is usually applied to qualifications and learning. Qualifications are graduate level (i.e. from graduate certificate to doctorate). When applied to learning, the term means learning of the highest level of complexity, breadth and detail.
VLE / Virtual Learning Environment	All universities have 'Virtual Learning Environments' which learners can access to support their studies. They will often have handbooks and other materials online. They can be accessed from any computer with web access. VLEs may also have specific tasks for you to undertake as part of your module or unit, and include blogs or other methods of communication between learners. You normally need to be a registered and enrolled learner to access these services.
Worker Researcher / Insider Researcher	A very important concept in WBL which recognises the importance of the WBL learner as both a worker and researcher. Its main importance is in relation to ethical dilemmas that might arise, and the relevance of knowledge the learner may develop in the workplace or professional setting.

Biographies of Contributors

Sue Bennett

Like many young people embarking on their careers, at that time I was unable to determine where my future lay and I took the 'sensible' route into business. I spent many years working in finance – long enough to know it wasn't for me! Not knowing what I wanted to do, whilst working I studied part-time for five years and achieved my Business Studies degree in my mid-thirties. I never looked back; I was hooked
on learning. Moving on, I found myself in the manufacturing sector in a human resources and training and development role, and realised that I was not only a lifelong learner myself, but I had a commitment to the development and education of others. I obtained my teaching qualifications and was self-employed for a number of years, teaching part time in Further Education, working with Apprenticeships and delivering bespoke training solutions to clients. Working in Higher Education was a natural progression and I now work for Northumbria University, within a team dedicated to supporting employer engagement and work-related learning.

Alan Durrant

My working life started at the age of fourteen when I worked weekends for my dad who was a silversmith. I repaired jewellery and I always remember that I was paid a proper adult wage but had to do good quality work to earn it! It was a good lesson, something I applied during my career in the jewellery industry as a designer, craftsman and manager. When I turned to teaching in the 1980s, I tried to transmit that same sense of worth to my students. I wanted my students to develop both professional skills *and* professional attitudes. Moving into WBL was an easy step because it has enabled me to work with established and establishing professionals to help them recognise the value of their skills, knowledge and attributes. This 'self-knowledge' is very important in WBL as it focuses individuals and employers on areas of strength, and indicates areas for further improvement of value to the individual and the employer. While I think that universities are still great places to prepare young people for skilled work, it is work based learning that will enable established workers and organisations to adapt to the rapidly changing world we are all experiencing.

Ann Minton

Upon reflection, WBL has been the foundation of my working life. Both Radiography and Ultrasound training involved working in a hospital alongside state registered professionals, whilst participating in a series of weekly master classes. Theoretical principles were learned and debated, and practice was critically reviewed; all skills that are fundamental for work based learners.

Ultrasound opened the door to the world of Assisted Conception, which has become a lifelong passion. Working at the cutting edge of this exciting field means that working and learning are inevitable. The skills I developed in healthcare practice are easily transferred to my current role supporting learners in a variety of workplace contexts. The development of bespoke learning solutions to meet client needs is also innovative, and requires the same passion and sense of humour. Both result in an exciting and fulfilling working life.

Chris Newman

My first degree was in History and Politics and followed by a Masters in Victorian Studies, in the days when there were grants rather than fees for higher education (yes – I am that old!). I went on to train to be a teacher and found that the subject specialism was less important to me than encouraging pupils to develop and achieve. Since those early teaching experiences, the main focus of my professional working life has been around developing learning, that of pupils and then of teachers, through initial training and in-service work, and of course my own personal learning as I faced new challenges through different job roles. I started tutoring negotiated work based learners in 2002, and have been hooked ever since. It is a privilege to see the creativity and resourcefulness of people who already have very full and sometimes complex lives, in all kinds of personal and job roles and work sectors, pushing themselves on to gain skills, knowledge, understanding and that all important piece of paper – qualifications, and the recognition and enhanced self-esteem which they bring. I count myself fortunate in seeing the commonalities and differences we all experience at work – even in the twilight of my career it still has the power to excite me.

Steve Partridge

As a trainee teacher in the mid 1970s, little did I know how some reading of radical education texts, which saw each student as a unique and rich source of learning rather than a passive recipient, would bring me full circle many years later. After several years as a junior school teacher, I moved into nursing, then into nurse education, where I was introduced by a link university to some highly creative, student-centred work which still strongly influences my thinking. After working as an APEL co-ordinator for some time, I moved into the independent health care sector to develop nursing practice and manage education and training services. My move into higher education at Middlesex University in London, where I am able to focus on WBL with a vast range of students, brings me back almost to my starting point. Each tutorial, be it with sports coaches, nurses or police officers, is a unique challenge as learning and development is unravelled and achievement is recognised and celebrated. Never a dull moment!

Alison Pringle

Alongside others working in this area, I've travelled a circuitous route to the field of work based learning. After ten years in banking I decided to study full-time, which took me to the University of Exeter for a degree in American and Commonwealth Arts. My first job after graduation was as a researcher on a World Music Project, which led to postgraduate study in the US. With a particular interest in music, obviously I was obliged to spend much research time over the next few years in the juke joints of the Deep South!

I developed an interest in workplace learning whilst teaching at Louisiana State University. Through a desire to give my students more meaningful assignments, I became involved in the development and teaching of 'service learning' programmes, which allow students to put their newly acquired academic skills into practice in 'real-life' community and other voluntary projects. Upon returning to the north of England I have worked at Sunderland and Northumbria Universities in the areas of Lifelong Learning and Work-based Learning and am currently at Northumbria University supporting WBL programme development across the University. And, dedicated soul that I am, I return to those juke joints with great regularity!

Garth Rhodes

After leaving sixth form in the early 70s with miserable A level results, having spent most of my time enjoying the social activities (including heated debates over a lunchtime pint in the pub at lunch on the important issues of the day, such as the school rules on the length of our hair and width of our bell-bottoms), I embarked on a career in social care. I took a job as a care worker in a school for children with physical disabilities but soon realised that without higher qualifications it was very unlikely that I would ever change the world. I scraped a place into teacher training college, not because I wanted to teach, but then this was one of the few ways you could train in community work. After spending three glorious years as a student challenging conventional approaches to teacher training, canoeing, surfing and generally enjoying myself, I was very fortunate to get a position as a volunteer in Southern Africa, where (with a huge amount of self-righteousness, naivety and youthful arrogance) I established an international work-camps association to foster community development projects. Returning to the UK, I worked in community work, then moved into youth and adult training where I became heavily involved in NVQs and competence-based training. During this time I did my MA in Educational Development which was a real challenge; balancing a part-time course with work and home life. Since 1993, I've worked at Northumbria University, developing its accreditation and work based learning portfolio. I'm passionate about negotiated work based learning, as I believe it offers many of us non-traditional learners the opportunity to learn in and through our work, to develop our higher-level thinking, enabling us to make changes that really matter.

Tracey White

My career history has been extremely diverse. Leaving school at the age of sixteen I tried my hand at a multitude of jobs, from manual labour to office work to managing pubs and hotels before moving into HGV class 1 lorry driving. I then went overseas for five years, once again drifting from one job to the next. Upon reflection I was gathering a wealth of experience and transferable skills which are both key to WBL, but I wasn't satisfied.

When I eventually realised that I needed a focus at the age of thirty-one, I went to university to do my first degree in Tourism and Spanish, which resulted in me working as a lecturer in the field of tourism. I continued developing my own education and my professional development and very quickly became involved as a tutor in WBL. This gave me the chance to help people coming from experienced work backgrounds and to share my experiences and skills. I undertook a Masters degree in WBL and am now a senior lecturer in WBL. Having gone through my own amazing learning journey I now enjoy helping others through their new experiences.

David Young

I've been a teacher for a long time – nearly 39 years in fact. During this time I've taught literally thousands of learners, from Reception Class infants to doctoral candidates and I've always been interested in what they thought about their learning. My PhD was about pupils' perspectives on the curriculum they were offered. Another career-long interest has been trying to get learners to write for real audiences, not just do exercises.

After working in schools and a local authority advisory service, in 1991 I joined Derbyshire College of Higher Education, now the University of Derby, where I'm Professor of Work-based Learning. I've been engaged in the development of award-bearing WBL in higher education since the mid-1990s and I've done lots of external examining, staff development and consultancy in the field in the UK and internationally. This is all interesting stuff, of course, but still the most exciting part of my professional life is working alongside work based learners – many of whom are as new to academic ways as they are skilled and experienced at work – as they begin to discover the real excellence of which many of them are capable. I think really that most of my early career was just about getting ready to be involved with them.

Further Reading

Billet, S, Fenwick, T and Somerville, M (eds) (2006) *Work, Subjectivity and Learning*, The Netherlands: Springer

Boud, D et al (eds) (1985) *Reflection. Turning experience into learning*, London: Kogan Page.

Boud, D and Solomon, N (eds) (2001) *Work Based Learning: a New Higher Education?*, Buckingham: SRHE & Open Univeraity Press

Burton J and Perkins J (2003) 'Accounts of personal learning in primary care', *Work Based Learning in Primary care*, 1, 19–32

Chapman L and Howkins E (2003) 'Work Based Learning: making a difference in practice', *Nursing Standard*, 17(34), 39–42

Cottrell, S (2003) *Skills for Success*, Basingstoke: Palgrave Macmillan

Cottrell, S (3rd ed. 2008) *The Study Skills Handbook*, Basingstoke: Palgrave Macmillan

Cunningham I, Dawes G and Bennet B (2005) *The Handbook of Work Based Learning*, Farnham: Gower

Dewey, J (1933) *How We Think*, New York: D C Heath

Evans, K, Hodgkinson, P, Rainbird, H and Unwin, L (2006) *Improving Workplace Learning*, London: Routledge

Flanagan J, Baldwin S and Clarke O (2000) 'Work-based learning as a means of developing and assessing nurse competence', *Journal of Advanced Nursing*, 9(3), 360–8

Garnett, J and Young, D (eds) (2008) *Work Based learning Futures II*, Bolton: University Vocational Awards Council

Kolb D (1984) *Experiential Learning*, London: Prentice Hall.

Raelin, J (2008) *Work-Based Learning: Bridging Knowledge and Action in the Workplace*, San Francisco: Jossey-Bass

Rainbird, H, Fuller, A and Munro, A (2004) *Workplace Learning in Context*, London: Routledge

Schon D (1987) *Educating the Reflective Practitioner*, San Francisco: Jossey-Bass

Young, D and Garnett, J (eds) (2007) *Work Based Learning Futures*, Bolton: University Vocational Awards Council

Levels of academic study

Below are detailed descriptors for each level:

Level 4 (Higher Education level 1; Certificates)

- Responsibility for courses of action and their results, including wider impacts;
- Thinking through and choosing courses of action;
- Coping effectively with a range of unfamiliar situations and problems;
- Recognising the implications of different issues and courses of action;
- Identifying and evaluating the practical effects and impact of operating parameters;
- Acting on understandings of relationships and contradictions between principles and ideas;
- Investigating, analysing and evaluating information to identify relationships and make informed judgements;
- Reinterpreting and combining information to develop ideas and choose courses of action or develop ways forward;
- Designing investigations to provide new information and affect practice, including through practical investigation;
- Evaluating the appropriateness of different approaches and their impacts;
- Producing own ideas and developing innovative responses;
- Developing novel solutions to problems.

Level 5 (Higher Education level 2; Foundation degrees and Diplomas)

- Responsibility across a broad area rather than for individual tasks, including for negotiating objectives and outcomes and for their wider impacts ;
- Developing thought-through courses of action;
- Coping effectively with a range of unfamiliar situations and problems;
- Understanding the implications of different issues and courses of action;
- Identifying dilemmas and value-conflicts;
- Identifying and evaluating the effects and impact of operating parameters and principles;
- Drawing on a broad personal or formal knowledge base and set of mental models relating to the area of practice;
- Developing practical theories, ideas and models including to find ways forward when faced with contradictions and gaps;
- Researching, analysing and evaluating information to identify relationships and patterns and make informed judgements;
- Designing practical research to provide new information and affect areas of practice;
- Evaluating the effects of options and actions, including impacts outside of the immediate context;
- Taking innovative approaches to address issues;
- Developing novel solutions to sets of problems.

Level 6 (Higher Education level 3; Ordinary and Honours degrees)

- Responsibility across a broad area including for planning, resourcing and quality as well as for outcomes and their immediate and wider impacts;
- Developing thought-through courses of action;
- Working effectively in complex and unpredictable contexts;
- Understanding the implications of different issues and courses of action;
- Understanding and managing dilemmas and value-conflicts;
- Identifying interrelationships between wider systems in which the area of practice is located;
- Drawing on a broad personal or formal knowledge-base and set of mental models relating to the area of practice;
- Developing and evaluating a range of practical theories, ideas and models, including to find ways forward in problematic situations;
- Researching, analysing and evaluating information to identify relationships and patterns and make informed judgements;
- Designing practical, methodologically sound research to provide new information and affect areas of practice ;
- Evaluating the actual and potential effects of theories and actions, including impacts outside of the immediate context ;
- Taking innovative approaches in complex situations;
- Developing novel approaches to systems.

Level 7 (Higher Education level 4; Postgraduate awards)

- Full responsibility for methods, actions and immediate and wider impacts which extend beyond the immediate area of practice;

- Developing thought-through courses of action which take into account issues beyond the immediate area of practice;

- Working effectively in problematic contexts which contain value-conflicts and uncertainties which extend beyond the immediate area of practice;

- Understanding alternative implications of different issues and courses of action;

- Understanding and managing dilemmas and value-conflicts;

- Understanding and acting on interrelationships between wider systems in which the area of practice is located;

- Using mastery of knowledge relating to, and extending into the wider context of, the area of practice;

- Developing and critically evaluating a range of practical theories, ideas and models, including to overcome dilemmas and find ways forward in problematic situations;

- Researching, analysing and evaluating information to identify interrelationships between wider systems in which the area of practice is located;

- Undertaking substantial investigation to address significant areas of practice, using methodologies which are consistent with their purposes and contexts;

- Critically evaluating thinking, action and structural factors operating in the area of practice, including underlying assumptions, and identifying implications for wider systems beyond the area of practice;

- Developing innovative ways forward in complex and unpredictable situations;

- Developing novel approaches to systems.

Level 8 (Higher Education level 5; Doctoral awards)

- Responsibility as a leading practitioner in a community of practice and extending beyond the immediate area of practice;
- Developing thought-through courses of action which take into account issues beyond the immediate area of practice;
- Working innovatively in problematic contexts and engaging with value conflicts and uncertainties which extend widely in and beyond the area of practice;
- Understanding alternative implications of different issues and courses of action;
- Understanding and managing dilemmas and value-conflicts in a way which takes forward wider practice;
- Understanding and acting on interrelationships between wider systems in which the area of practice is located;
- Using critical and creative mastery of a broad range of concepts, theories and practices and the assumptions underlying them from perspectives which transcend individual disciplines and contexts;
- Developing and critically evaluating a range of practical theories, ideas and models, including to overcome structural dilemmas and find ways forward in problematic situations;
- Researching, analysing and evaluating information to identify interrelationships between wider systems in which the area of practice is located;
- Generating new understandings and approaches which extend or redefine existing knowledge and practice;
- Undertaking original investigation to address significant areas of practice, using methodologies which are practically and philosophically consistent with their wider purposes and contexts;
- Critically evaluating thinking, action and structural factors operating in the area of practice, including underlying assumptions, and identifying implications for wider systems beyond the area of practice;
- Developing innovative approaches which redefine or extend the scope of practice;
- Developing novel approaches to complexes of systems.